Praise for *Anyone Can*

'I have seen Simon's strategic innova
for its huge impact. The reason this ᴸᵒᵒ...
beyond the innovation practices normally discussed into the difficult
but essential work of building alliances and driving implementation.
It also covers both government and business in deeply insightful ways
that will be helpful in navigating the years ahead.'

Jon Huntsman, former two times Governor of Utah;
US Ambassador to China and Russia; board member,
Ford Motors; Deputy Chairman, Mastercard

'Anyone can innovate but few realise it. This beautiful collection of
patterns and recipes from a seasoned innovation leader is an ode to
"you can do it".'

Anne Lange, serial tech entrepreneur and investor;
currently on the Boards of Inditex, Orange,
Pernod-Ricard and Peugeot Invest

'This book is a direct blow to the myth of the solo entrepreneur that
currently operates in most public and private institutions. It also suggests, from real experience, concrete alternatives for building a real
model of disruptively inclusive innovation.'

Dr Gorka Espiau Idoiaga, Director of the Innovation Centre,
the University of the Basque country and Columbia University;
former senior advisor to the Basque President

'Simon is one of those rare individuals who not only understands and
drives innovation but has successfully done so across multiple organisations, creating extensive ecosystems of impact. Equally unique
is his ability to reflect deeply, discerning patterns and tracing their
evolution as they transform over time. This book is invaluable.'

Indy Johar, co-founder, Dark Matter Labs and
Urban Practice Architecture

'A thoughtful and provocative route map to effective innovation strategies by an incredible leader and practitioner.'

Relina Bulchandani, Executive Vice President, Workplace, Salesforce

'*Anyone Can Innovate* is a charming guide to driving a dynamic approach to innovation at the individual level, which is a key piece of the larger puzzle of strengthening the innovation ecosystem. Simon explicitly touches on this larger framework as well, and effectively makes the case that innovation is done collectively, and is a product of ecosystems (not just individuals) in which public and private sector actors work together in a symbiotic way.'

Professor Mariana Mazzucato, Professor in the Economics of Innovation and Public Value, University College London; founding director of the UCL Institute for Innovation and Public Purpose

Anyone Can Innovate

Pearson

At Pearson, we have a simple mission: to help people
make more of their lives through learning.

We combine innovative learning technology with trusted
content and educational expertise to provide engaging
and effective learning experiences that serve people
wherever and whenever they are learning.

From classroom to boardroom, our curriculum materials, digital
learning tools and testing programmes help to educate millions
of people worldwide – more than any other private enterprise.

Every day our work helps learning flourish, and
wherever learning flourishes, so do people.

To learn more, please visit us at **www.pearson.com**

Anyone Can Innovate

Your step-by-step guide to inclusive innovation

Simon Willis

Pearson

Harlow, England • London • New York • Boston • San Francisco • Toronto • Sydney
Dubai • Singapore • Hong Kong • Tokyo • Seoul • Taipei • New Delhi
Cape Town • São Paulo • Mexico City • Madrid • Amsterdam • Munich • Paris • Milan

PEARSON EDUCATION LIMITED
KAO Two
KAO Park
Harlow CM17 9NA
United Kingdom
Tel: +44 (0)1279 623623
Web: www.pearson.com

First edition published 2025 (print and electronic)

Pearson Education is not responsible for the content of third-party internet sites.

ISBN: 978-1-292-73616-7 (print)
          978-1-292-46810-5 (ePub)

British Library Cataloguing-in-Publication Data
A catalogue record for the print edition is available from the British Library

Library of Congress Cataloging-in-Publication Data
A catalog record for the print edition is available from the Library of Congress

10 9 8 7 6 5 4 3 2 1
29 28 27 26 25

Cover design by Nick Redeyoff

Print edition typeset in 10/14 Charter ITC Pro by Straive
Printed in the UK by Bell and Bain Ltd, Glasgow

NOTE THAT ANY PAGE CROSS REFERENCES REFER TO THE PRINT EDITION

To the memory of Diogo Vasconcellos 1968–2011
'We have to fix the future.'

Contents

—

Author's acknowledgements

———

My sincere thanks to those who made comments or suggestions on earlier drafts. To the extent that any mistakes, flawed inferences or gratuitous insults remain in the text, I would look to blame these people before all others:

Olaoluwa Abagun, Bronte Adams, Maria Aguado, Gary Bridge, Anthony Butts, Eloise Cook, Jeremy Crump, Professor Glyn Davis AC, Steve Effingham, Gorka Espiau, Bridget Farmer, Jacinda Humphry, Paul Johnston, Grant Johnstone, Asuka Kobayashi, Eric Laqueche, Jessie Lu, Daniel Nieto, Adrian Preston, Itziar Moreno, Amira Rashid, Cynthia Saab, Martin Stewart-Weeks, Louis Willis, Dimitri Zenghelis, May Zhang.

About the author

Simon grew up in Australia and worked as both an opera singer and an apprentice pastry chef, before moving to London to be a barman and roller-skating, singing, telegram deliverer. After several years working for the Quakers and Amnesty International he wangled his way into Oxford, where he took a first-class degree in PPE at Balliol College.

Simon then worked for a decade as a fast stream civil servant at the Department of Work and Pensions, Motability and Her Majesty's Treasury, where he led the financial crime branch representing the UK at G7, OECD and European negotiations leading to the inclusion of tax evasion as a predicate offence for money laundering.

He then moved to the private sector working on fraud detection software at Unisys before joining Cisco Systems, where for many years he ran first the European and then global public sector innovation practices as part of their legendary Internet Business Solutions Group. After periods of innovation leadership at two Silicon Valley startups and as CEO of the Young Foundation, he joined Mastercard as Vice President of Government innovation partnerships.

He is married and has four grown up children, two cats and a small fluffy dog called Yoshimi.

Introduction

———

'For it is said that humans are never satisfied, that you give them one thing and they want something more. And this is said in disparagement, whereas it is one of the greatest talents the species has and one that has made it superior to animals that are satisfied with what they have.'[1]

John Steinbeck

It was around 10 am on a cool September morning in North Carolina. Bridget Farmer hauled her wiry 5'3" frame out of her John Deere tractor and strode towards her farmhouse, oblivious of the stunning Autumnal surroundings. She was deep in thought. On reaching her back deck she paused and pulled a small, battered Nokia phone from her well-worn Harris tweed jacket with the beige suede elbow patches. She liked the Nokia because she didn't use most social networks and its battery lasted 5 days, whereas her iPhone invariably needed recharging long before the sun had set. Squinting at the rugged Carolinian horizon she came to a decision, folded her scratched Ray-bans into her jacket pocket and dialled a familiar number.

'I've read the first draft of your innovation essay Simon.'

'What do you think?' I replied nervously.

'OK, so a couple of things. I like it.'

She didn't need to articulate the 'but'.

'Remember most business books are just good articles that have been pumped full of hot air until they're book length.'

She'd shared this theory often.

'You have enough ideas for a book but it's just a short book.'

I agreed.

'There's nothing wrong with short books. Short books are good and some of them are great.'

I started thinking about *A Vindication of the Rights of Women* by Mary Wollstonecraft when she interrupted and said,

'Think of Strunk & White. Started life at 43 pages and never went much over 100. It's enough. But I'm going to give a few pointers to follow if you feel like it.

Firstly, don't put little bite-sized summaries in shaded boxes. We aren't children – don't infantilise your readers.'

I agreed.

'Secondly, don't try to summarise complex thoughts into 3-point or 10-point lists that all start with the same letter. It's a complex subject and the people who read it and get value from it will be intelligent grown-ups, not 14-year-olds, ok?

Thirdly, don't include case studies that don't have a point. And particularly don't include case studies that are obviously spinning companies or governments you've been paid by or hope to be paid by. It is transparently inauthentic and egregiously annoying. If you're going to include some of your own case studies, and I know you have many, I'd tend to go more with the failures.'

I agreed to all her requests, wondering just how small this book could grow.

'And finally', she said, increasing her vocal font-size, 'Don't start any chapters with a homely little human story about some woman at 10 am on a crisp Autumn morning, doing blah blah blah. You aren't writing for the *New York Times* and just because we are in business, doesn't mean we have the attention span of guppies.'

I agreed with all her conditions.

But I had one final question:

'That's all ok Bridget. But who are you?'

She laughed.

'You should know Simon. You invented me.'

How to use this book

The structure of this book is very simple. It presents innovation in five main steps: clearing the ground (first two chapters), establishing your true objective (Chapter 3), creativity (Chapter 4), building alliances for adoption (Chapter 5) and implementation (Chapter 6).

Chapter 1 – What the hell is innovation anyway?

I start by clearing the ground, laying out what innovation is and how it is different from other things. This chapter doesn't have the many useful patterns and examples of the following chapters so you can skip it if you want but I think it's useful to know what you are trying to do.

Chapter 2 – What do people keep getting wrong about it?

I continue with a brief survey of the myths, misunderstandings and deliberate misdirection that pervade the area, a guide for the unwary with practical suggestions on how to set out on your journey and avoid the common pitfalls.

Chapter 3 – Get your motivations straight and you're half way there

This chapter looks at the intentions of innovators and the relationship between their intentions and their probability of success. I argue, among other things, that successful innovation is rooted both in the exercise of free will and a respect for the free choices of others.

Chapter 4 – Post-it notes aren't enough – getting creative

This chapter and the following two form the practical heart of the book, grouping the patterns of successful innovation strategies into three broad and overlapping stages: creation, adoption and implementation. Chapter 6 is all about creation, having crazy ideas and freeing yourself up from the doomed assumptions of determinism.

Chapter 5 – Build alliances or all your work is wasted

Creation is fundamental, but far from being enough if you really want to change some aspect of the world. This chapter looks at the often forgotten but fundamental art of getting your idea adopted by those colleagues, funders, stakeholders and decision makers you need on board if you have any hope of success.

Chapter 6 – Implementation – now comes the hard graft!

This chapter on implementation also dwells at length on issues of organisational culture, team composition, leadership and management. The obstacles to innovation are many, but these are among the most fundamental.

Chapter 7 – 60 Propositions

A summary for the impatient and a manifesto for the passionate. In this chapter I have sought to distil the fundamental points made in the rest of the book in as brief and succinct a way as possible. My aim is that this short list of propositions could be used both as a reminder or a refresher but also as a possible cheat-sheet or wall poster for those organising workshops, ideations sessions, working groups, task forces, etc.

Chapter 8 – 23 ½ Workshop outlines

A set of simple, practical workshop outlines that allow you to explore, get comfortable with and apply the patterns, approaches and insights of the previous chapters. These run from one or two hours to a full day and may be adjusted or combined depending on the ambitions of the users or facilitator.

The purpose of this book is to provide a basic toolkit for those who wish to innovate in their company, department, agency or charity. And some guidance for their leaders and policy makers. It is based on my profound belief that innovation is not just too important to be left to experts but that it has rarely been done by experts. It can generally only be done by passionate and diverse groups of people who share a desire to improve something in the world. It is also my intention to inspire people to try this. Reading business books can be one of the most mind-crushingly tedious experiences you can have in life, and the many books on innovation are no exception. Probably because most are written by academics and journalists who have next to no idea how hard it is to innovate in real life, how to manage bizarrely diverse groups, corral strangely elusive resources and defend, survive or conceal failure after failure. It is particularly odd that innovation books should be so boring because, I promise you, this subject is deeply human – full of drama, excitement, conflict, strangeness, beauty, humour, politics, anger and desire. Business academics and management consultants have drained it of all humanity. It is part of my purpose to fight back. My ineffable old friend Steve has pointed out that there are really three voices at play in the book. The first is empirical and practical and it pursues the main objective, which is to give practical advice based on real experience. The second is passionate and angry and speaks what I believe to be hard truths about the lamentable state of management and leadership in most of our companies, agencies, departments and charities. I could have deleted much of this without detracting from the practical objectives, but I left it in because it's more fun that way and may even be useful for some. The third intervenes from time to time to look at the theory, political philosophy and economics of innovation. I wanted to see if there is a structured underpinning for my ragbag of claims. And I now believe there is. Feel free to skip easily recognisable musings if you just want to get to the practical heart of the matter.

Most of us lack permission to think at work, and when we become senior enough to give ourselves permission, we have no time. Our work time is filled with a howling of process, politics and pretence signifying self-promotion. I want to help you change that, whether you are a frustrated innovator or aspire to be that most rare of corporate animals, the visionary senior manager, leader or politician.

You may think that your organisation will welcome your aspiration to innovate. This would be understandable given that they have almost certainly regularly broadcast their devotion to the importance of innovation in pursuing profits, impact or true customer or citizen service. But I have some very sad news for you. The fetishisation of innovation in late capitalism is all about defending the rent-seeking and price gouging of the few at the expense of the very many. Try actually doing innovation in your organisation and you will likely as not quickly find yourself in deep trouble. For this and other reasons, progressives have turned their backs on the whole subject, supposing that it is the work of the neo-liberal devil. Which may explain how they have gone from changing the world for the better a century ago to changing almost nothing (including, catastrophically, most real-terms incomes) for many decades now. That's why this book is called *Anyone can innovate*. It is partly motivated by a profound interest in why everyone says they love innovation and then make your life extremely difficult when you try it. Perhaps it is partly because it is subversive by its very nature. The people more senior than you have benefited from the current status quo by definition. As Machiavelli said, 'There is nothing more perilous to conduct … than to take the lead in the introduction of a new order of things. Because the innovator has for enemies all those who have done well under the old conditions, and lukewarm defenders in those who may do well under the new.'[2] Innovating is natural human behaviour, an expression of the desire to improve things. When they tell you that you don't have the skills, the remit or the right to innovate they are lying. Anyone can innovate.

This is not a blueprint, a set of processes or a recipe for innovation. It is a tentative set of overlapping patterns and some simple tools and exercises that have provably worked for me and the many teams I have worked with. They should give you enough conceptual orientation to develop your own innovation project or movement.

A word or two about the difference between patterns and processes, which is explored more deeply in Chapter 1. Patterns are the raw material of observable behaviour. Processes are a higher level of explanation of raw patterns. By focussing on patterns, we give permission to ourselves to broaden the scope of our creativity and free ourselves from the hidden assumptions, limits and prescriptions inherent in all processes and recipes. The religious devotion to process as a substitute for thought prevalent in most organisations perhaps mitigates risk in the short run but surely guarantees organisational death in the end.

Professional groups are like exclusive clubs, very keen on mystification, codification, complex process and arcane language. Like little boys' clubs they build hiding places in the woods or 'cubbies in the bush' as we would say in Australia. In England they used to be called guilds, professions and gentlemen's clubs. Innovation isn't like that and never has been. Everyone can participate in it at certain times and places. This book aims to give you some of the things you need to know about purpose, place, people and paterns, timing, hacks, systems and structures, as well as leadership and management. It is based on some good research by others and the practical innovation work that my friends, colleagues, and I have done over the last 30 years.

Notes

1 The *Pearl*, John Steinbeck, 1947.
2 Machiavelli, *The Prince*, 1532.

chapter 1

What the hell is innovation anyway?

'Every creative idea has a history, but not necessarily a reason for being.'[1]

Ferran Adrià

Innovation is the sustainable, purpose-driven answer to a previously unsolved problem in the world. It is typically conducted by a close-knit but diverse group of people united by their desire to improve the world in a particular way, informed by their understanding of the painfully unmet needs of real people. It brings together already existing elements, products, patterns and people in an iterative series of trade-offs between financial, social, political and physical constraints in a way that leads to the creation, adoption and implementation of a new approach. All three of these stages – creation, adoption and implementation – are critical. A lot has been written about the first stage, about creation, ideation, design and invention. But without adoption, there is no implementation and without implementation, there is no innovation. Just pilots, daydreams, stories and hype.

Innovation is by its nature disruptive because, in changing the way organisations solve a problem or set of problems, it changes the way the organisations that adopt it work as well as changing the way some people live their lives. It opens up new possibilities, often unlocking radically more productive or profitable approaches. It always gives expression to a purpose, whether that is more free time, more productive or enriching work, a longer or more healthy life, more pleasurable ways to eat or play or dress or socialise, faster or safer ways to travel, more harmonious or just ways for people to live together, new ways to learn and so on, ad infinitum and beyond.

Perhaps because of this, it transpires that the management of innovation work and the working methods required to do it successfully are also disruptive of the day-to-day norms, working methods and hierarchies of our companies, government departments and agencies and civil society organisations, including charities and political parties. It seems inevitable, therefore that innovators will meet resistance, opposition and aggression, even in organisations passionately convinced of the need for innovation. This makes it tactically and emotionally difficult work to do. Being punished or excluded for trying to do something your organisation is passionately devoted to in theory and desperately needs to do in practice is an unpleasant feeling to say the least. I imagine it's like being hit by a pacifist when still a child or discovering that your Prime Minister threw weekly bring-a-bottle shindigs throughout lockdown.

Learning to deal with this, to navigate it and overcome it is therefore of paramount importance. And it turns out that success in navigating adoption and implementation and the myriad barriers encountered is rooted in the approach we take to invention. There is much at stake here, because the company that stops innovating will die and the government that stops innovating will lose the trust of the people it serves. The challenges we face from globalisation, the climate catastrophe and environmental degradation, growing inequality, pandemics, lack of productivity, stagnant wages, automation and artificial intelligence (AI) and an apparent reduction in the legitimacy of and trust in our institutions, companies and civil society organisations will never be solved without innovation. It is truly important that we get better at this.

Innovation has elements of invention, discovery, creativity, entrepreneurship, design, movement making and project-management, but it is none of these things. An invention is generally a new combination of existing elements but may have no impact on the world, no matter how good it is. Think of Betamax, the Dvorak keyboard layout or twentieth-century electric cars. A discovery makes apparent what was hidden but does nothing about the subsequent uses and recombination possible. Think of DNA, gravitational waves, dark matter and penicillin. Creativity may express a truth for the creator but says nothing about who may see or hear the creation and the effects it will have in the world. Think of the Taj Mahal, a Brett Whitely self-portrait or Lizzo's 'Juice'. Entrepreneurship builds a sustainable business model around an idea, but the idea need not be new. Think of Facebook, the Gap or Huawei. Design, or at least good design, is (to paraphrase Dieter Rams) the art and craft of trading off various constraints to create useful, aesthetically appealing, understandable, new things, services and processes. Think of Robert Best's Bestlite desk lamp, Coco Chanel's Boy Bag or Interactive Wayfinding by Southwest Airlines.

It will be immediately apparent that one of the distinctive features of innovation is that it is rarely carried out by one person or one group – it is more akin to an iterative, networked movement, often moving back and forth over sectoral boundaries through complex chains of innovation. For example, from not-for-profit groups to the public sector to various companies and back again or even inside a single company from product to sales to business development to finance to leadership and back again. One of the most interesting, failed innovation projects I worked on was the Planetary Skin Initiative, which is discussed below. It endeavoured to ground truth satellite imagery with exemplary ground sensors to allow algorithmic interpretation of visual satellite data in a way that would provide close to real-time tracking of carbon stocks and flows across the entire surface of the planet, initially motivated by the need to monetise non-deforestation.[2] It involved a flow of work from several private sector companies to NASA to several universities to several state and national governments and back again. This will be an increasingly required approach as we tackle the big issues that face us, and some ways to get it right are discussed below.

Most studies of innovation methods have tended to focus on just private entrepreneurialism and start-ups, or just innovation or intra-preneurialism in larger companies or just public sector innovation, or just social or civic innovation or just urban innovation, etc. There is nothing wrong with this approach and many good hacks, methods and case studies have been uncovered and documented. But I am more interested in trying to uncover the deep common themes between them as well as the many things they might be able to learn from each other. It's not just a hunch or an observation that cross sectoral study of innovation will be most fruitful in revealing deep common patterns – it's the nature of innovation itself. Or to put it really simplistically, multi-disciplinary university departments win more Nobel prizes than specialised institutes just as Nobel prize winning breakthroughs have more interdisciplinary effect than specialised effect.[3] Needless to say, most science funding continues to largely ignore this pattern.

There is, however, an even deeper reason why it might be beneficial to look at the three main sectors (private, public and not for profit) as a whole. Recent groundbreaking work by Mariana Mazzucato, professor and founder of University College London's Institute for Innovation and Public Purpose, has made a very strong case for the idea that we should stop looking exclusively to the private sector for models of successful innovation.[4] Further, that many of the key innovations we depend on have actually come into existence because of the patient, early and long-term investment the public sector excels in. In fact, it becomes clear in the light of her work that it is often the *combination* or emergent collaboration of and between the sectors that has led to so many key breakthroughs, not just in pharmaceuticals and the digital world, but in transport, logistics, clean energy, cars, market platforms, military, finance systems, construction and so on. Whether we are looking at the role of NASA in developing the digital camera and subsequent CMOS sensor miniaturisation now featuring ubiquitously in mobile telephones, the New York Port Authority in supporting early containerisation, the role of DARPA in the early Internet or the role of the $5 billion + of loans, investments, tax breaks and grants to Tesla before 2015 and $billions in EV subsidies since,[5] the impact of the sectors working together is everywhere around us. The reasons why the private sector beneficiaries of this might exhibit such consistent bad faith and ingratitude to their less well remunerated collaborators is mysterious.

Finally, it is becoming clearer now that we need governments to regulate extensively and dynamically for innovation to flourish. In a thousand different areas from the protection of labour as traditional approaches and protections become disintermediated or arbitraged by new platforms, to the proper functioning of markets, the depredations of financialisation and the offshore, and the emerging political dangers and platform monopolisation by the big tech companies, now accelerated by unregulated AI.

Father of modern innovation theory, the Austrian economist and sociologist, Joseph Schumpeter understood, as almost no economists had before and remarkably few since, what role innovation played in our well-being and the central role of the entrepreneur in capitalism. His most famous book was *Capitalism, Socialism and Democracy* (1947):

'So is the history of the productive apparatus of the iron and steel industry from the charcoal furnace to our own type of furnace, or the history of the apparatus of power production from the overshot water wheel to the modern power plant, or the history of transportation from the mail-coach to the airplane. The opening up of new markets, foreign or domestic, and the organisational development from the craft shop and factory to such concerns as U.S. Steel illustrate the same process of industrial mutation – if I may use that biological term – that incessantly revolutionises the economic structure *from within*, incessantly destroying the old one, incessantly creating a new one. This process of Creative Destruction is the essential fact about capitalism. It is what capitalism consists in and what every capitalist concern has to live in . . . But in capitalist reality as distinguished from it's textbook picture, it is not [just price, quality and sales effort] which counts but the competition from the new commodity, the new technology, the new source of supply, the new type of organisation . . . competition which commands a decisive cost or quality advantage and which strikes, not at the margins of the profits and the outputs of the existing firms but at their foundations and their very lives.'[6]

It is extraordinary to consider that Professor Mazzucato is one of relatively few economists since Schumpeter to appreciate the central role of innovation in a thriving society. Paul Romer, Michael Porter and a small handful of others are exceptions. Mazzucato is both institutionally and intellectually directly descended from Schumpeter by way of her University of Sussex predecessors, SPRU founder Chris Freeman, a pioneer of neo-Schumpeterian innovation technology and growth theory and his student and beloved, Venezuelan British thinker, Professor Carlotta Perez, author of the extraordinary *Technological Revolutions and Financial Capital*,[7] which takes forward Schumpeter's theories on Kondratiev waves and dynamic growth cycles.

The political economy of innovation is still nascent but there are positive signs beyond the work of Perez and Mazzucato. Former Cato institute thinker and writer Will Wilkinson, who has been drifting leftwards towards the centre right for some time now, is not the only one who has made the potentially significant observation that the preservation of Schumpeterian creative destruction in a democracy probably requires a reasonably strong welfare state to cushion its inevitable negative social effects.[8] And to pay for that we need a thriving economy, which in turn may depend on reasonably unfettered creative destruction. Coming slowly to an analogous conclusion (but empowered by a more or less complete ignorance of social welfare systems) are some of the tech bros who have recently fallen in love with basic income guarantee schemes of various kinds. Never mind the dignity of work as a central contribution to fulfilment in life – just give everyone a precariously small amount to live on so we can get on with concentrating virtually all the wealth created by the worker bees in a few dozen pairs of hands. I consider below just how unfettered creative destruction might 'reasonably' be. But clearly this set of tensions between the sources of growth and their negative social effects has been one of the defining political fault-lines in developed economies for the last 40 years.

The designer, architect and philosopher Christopher Alexander and his colleagues published *A Pattern Language* in 1977 and with typical perversity, the introduction to it, '*The Timeless Way of Building*,' 2 years later. It tackles the design of buildings and places as a series of problems solved with design elements that interact and are iterated towards an optimal but imperfect solution to a design problem. Yet animated by a mysterious and difficult-to-define element that coheres towards meaning and beauty in a place, the thing with no name. Although in his later work this nameless element could be defined as 'livingness' or the quality of being life enhancing.

'It is a process through which the order of a building or a town grows out directly from the inner nature of the people, and the animals, and plants and matter which are in it. It is process which allows the life inside a person, or a family, or a town, to flourish, openly, in freedom, so vividly that it gives birth, of its own accord to the natural order which is needed to sustain life.[9] (TWB, p. 7)

This is why it is so easy for others to play on our fears. They can persuade us that we must have more method, and more system, because we are afraid of our own chaos. Without method and more method, we are afraid the chaos which is in us will reveal itself. And yet these methods only make things worse.

The fact is that the difference between a good building and a bad building, between a good town and a bad town, is an objective matter. It is the difference between health and sickness, wholeness and dividedness, self-maintenance and self-destruction.'

This conceptual framework or philosophical approach has been used by others in various fields. *Fearless Change: Patterns for Introducing New Ideas* by Linda Rising and Mary Lynn Manns[10] looks at a series of disruptive change agents from history to codify simple patterns for driving change in resistant organisations. *Compendium for a Civic Economy* by Indy Johar's 00 Group[11] looks at 25 patterns derived from working case studies in urban regeneration and community building. An earlier example from the software field is provided by *Design Patterns: Elements of Reusable Object-Oriented Software* by 'the gang of four', Erich Gamma, Richard Helm, Ralph Johnson and John Vlissides,[12] which has been followed by multiple software pattern compendia in OOP, C++, Java and others, although the need for many early patterns was obviously eliminated by subsequent language developments and now at accelerating pace by AI. The OOPSLA community explicitly referenced Alexander as their influence and invited him to keynote their 1996 conference in San Jose, which is well worth watching.[13]

Although he likely would not claim it, I would argue that one of the most important innovation books of recent times, *Thinking Fast and Slow* by Daniel Kahneman,[14] is also built along similar conceptual lines. The bulk of that book focusses on the less-than-fully-rational heuristics we use to make quick judgements. Biases caused by framing and anchoring, availability of information, loss aversion, etc. build a set of patterns of thought that undermine traditional confidence in the rationality of human decision making in normal day-to-day circumstances. The individual patterns are discovered by empirical research and practice, not determined by conceptual logic. We could easily imagine new heuristics being added to the list; for example, the tendency to find believable the claims of someone who has power over us or determines our financial well-being (and to laugh loudly at their jokes) or to believe in fairy tales that are in our financial interests to believe like doubting the link between fossil fuels and climate change or believing that immigrants supress wages or that trickle-down economics works.

The point of the pattern language approach is to create a shared and growing set of elements that can be built on, refined and added to by practitioners. It creates a language for collaboration and mutual education between people of very different outlooks, political views, professional training and objectives and purposes but it also proposes a philosophy to animate this collaboration, a philosophy which itself espouses collaboration in the pursuit of human flourishing. This approach is therefore consistent with itself and with its practice as well as with its intentions. Too often we have seen the various aspects of innovation practice start to be pushed into deadening processes and formulaic prescriptions by those who wish to profit from it without understanding it, those who understand its importance but don't understand how to do it, those who theorise but have never practiced and those who are perhaps unknowingly afraid of the human wildness at its heart. '. . . we are afraid of our own chaos . . .'. This book is a starting point in an attempt to elaborate an alternative approach.

Notes

1   Adrià, ADAE, 2008, p. 56.

2   https://www.fastcompany.com/3024393/how-nasa-cisco-and-a-tricked-out-planetary-skin-could-make-the-world-a-sa

3   https://www.researchgate.net/figure/The-disciplinary-interdisciplinary-impact-of-Nobel-Prize-winning-discoveries-a_fig1_328671380

    https://theconversation.com/nobel-prizes-most-often-go-to-researchers-who-defy-specialization-winners-are-creative-thinkers-who-synthesize-innovations-from-varied-fields-and--even-hobbies-186193

4   Mazzucato, TES, Anthem, 2013.

5   https://www.latimes.com/business/la-fi-hy-musk-subsidies-20150531-story.html

6   Schumpeter, CSD, 1947, pp. 83–84.

7   Perez, TRAFC, Edward Elgar, 2002.

8   https://www.vox.com/2016/9/1/12732168/economic-freedom-score-america-welfare-state

9   Alexander, TWB, p. 15.

10 Rising, FC, 2004.

11 Johar, CFACE, 2011.

12 Gamma, DP, 1994.

13 https://www.youtube.com/watch?v=98LdFA-_zfA

14 Kahneman, TFAS, 2011.

chapter 2

What do people keep getting wrong about it?

'Some people see things that are and ask, why? Some people dream of things that never were and ask, why not?

Some people have to go to work and don't have time for all that.'

George Carlin[1]

Early education for all members of any new, growing or virtual team in the nature and strategies of innovation can be useful as many people have strange and misguided ideas and their senior managers are generally the worst. For reasons addressed in the last chapter on implementation, very few people ascended to senior management by being innovative. Either way, you will need to try to break down the misunderstandings that pervade the subject.

1 *Innovation is about making a thing or product.* In fact, there is no aspect of an organisation's business, operations, financing, approach to customers and citizens, communications, or relationship to suppliers and partners that cannot valuably be the subject of innovation. We perhaps have a picture of an iPhone in our minds and even then many of the innovations that have made iPhones successful are hard to see at first glance. Think about the App store. This platform innovation creates an incentivised global marketplace of programmers to bring features to an otherwise closed and vertically integrated product, which itself is the wrapping for dozens of previous innovations, including the iPod and iTunes. The iPod, in turn, was a wrapper for a package of innovations which together with iTunes turned a form factor innovation into a platform innovation derived from the P2P streaming innovations of Napster, KaZaH, etc. Even after all that, the iPhone is marketed in a retail innovation cluster crystallised in the Apple store, the highest sales per square foot of any retail outlet in history,[2] including mobile point of sale customer service innovations in a setting featuring characteristically high-spec glass and steel design, almost as if Apple still loved, respected and desired its customers.

There are many typologies and maps of innovation sub-categories, but the area is confused and contested. For our purposes, the following 21 simple categories will suffice: Product, platform, business model, channels to market, supply chain, employment, materials, service, marketing, branding, sales, organisational and institutional design, decision-making, recruitment, management, assessment, market structure, customer and citizen needs assessment, impact assessment and prototyping. No doubt there are others.

A practical exercise in this area is to do a 'no product brainstorming'. The facilitator identifies the obvious product innovation in the area under discussion and bans that as a subject of enquiry. You then break into groups and compete to see how many non-product areas you can identify, where innovation might carry the organisation forward. Don't be scared to include management, appraisal, incentives, recruitment, internal communications and so on. Vote on the top one to three areas and then compete to come up with the best list of wild ideas. Then each group gets to plagiarise one other group's idea and workshop it for a half day or two. Outlines for workshops based on this exercise and many others are in Chapter 8. Internal plagiarism lies at the heart of good group brainstorming as it does with innovation in large organisations more generally. More tips are given below on the huge power of deliberately and carefully giving away credit without completely shooting yourself in the foot.

2   *Innovators are special individuals.* We are still very much in the grip of the pervasive myth of the inventor. The Hollywoodisation of creation stories by company marketing departments has been further exacerbated by the corporatisation of Hollywood itself. We love stories of heroic individuals and this fits so well with the archetypal film script or 'narratological monomyth', so beautifully explained by Joseph Campbell in *The Hero's Journey*.[3]

But the reality of innovation has been further obscured by billionaire Silicon Valley founders who, perhaps unconsciously, express a need for heroic stories to explain why they aren't paying their taxes or workers properly. The dolorous effects of meritocracy warned of by Michael Young in his more or less completely misunderstood 1958 masterpiece, *The Rise of the Meritocracy*, mean that following the neoliberal turn in around 1980, we have increasingly inverted the idea that wealth and status should follow merit and have come to believe instead that merit comes from or is implied by wealth – which is therefore deserved.

Those who benefit from this obvious untruth have increasingly had the power and resource to amplify it with stark consequences for distorted industrial policy and wider political interventions that have entrenched and defended rising inequality.

In fact, virtually all interesting innovation is done by groups and ecosystems and *diversity* of perspective and experience is fundamental.[4] The bizarre culture wars around diversity, equity and inclusion (DEI) that disfigure the American media landscape in recent years more or less always miss the fundamental point that each element of DEI is fundamental to effective groups and teams that need to innovate. Which is most groups and teams.

A really useful exercise for you to try early in your innovation journey is to work backwards from the perfect team needed to the present composition. In other words, *innovate your innovation team first.* Challenge yourselves to imagine the perfect set of skills and experiences for the challenges ahead. Then map them against what you have and articulate the gaps. Sometimes the addition or co-option or borrowing of just one or two people to the team can plug a critical set of gaps, with potentially significant impact. If customers or citizens or other key users are involved in making your innovation a success, seriously ask yourself if you have people in your innovation group who know all the key customer/citizen segments from the inside. Don't be the NASA group that almost sent Sally Ride to space with 100 tampons for a six-day trip. You could run this exercise more than once. You are bound to have missed some relevant skills.

Some people also use random selection of members of a temporary or project-based innovation group. And there's nothing wrong with that as a way of eliminating selection biases of various kinds. It certainly has an increasingly respectable and well researched role to play in various forms of citizen democracy and its analogues. But it's not such a new idea. The Athenians used it to staff key juries and decision-making committees as a guard against the corrupting influence of oligarchy on democracy, an insight we seem to have lost touch with.

But the problem with random selection for a group being given a mission-critical task is legitimacy; not only their own sense of what they can do but the way others in the organisation regard them, particularly important during the innovation stages of adoption and implementation discussed in the following chapters.

One way around this, which I've found both valuable and productive, is to create a special test and then tell the chosen members of your taskforce that a combination of their answers to the test and their manager and peer feedback has identified them as being uniquely suitable to belong to a breakthrough task force because of their particular creative skills. Don't worry about analysing the test results. I have to tell you that this works beautifully to frame the right state of mind for a high-performing group. It has the same effect as telling a randomly chosen sales group that they are the sales elite team; repeated experiments have shown that they immediately and measurably outperform other sales teams with the same tasks and targets by 15 +per cent. That's all you need to know, by the way, about why you should immediately abandon all performance appraisal systems that tell 80 per cent of your staff that they aren't in the top group: a piece of collective management insanity that remains mysteriously prevalent in all but the most enlightened organisations outside of tech and consulting.[5]

At Mastercard they systematised the diverse innovation team-building step by setting up a directory of people with skills and experiences and some time to give to others' projects. They call it, appropriately, 'Unlocked'. It went underused for quite a long time because most people are too busy to think and it has to be driven by authentic leadership, perhaps backed up with real incentives, rather than offered as an interesting option. When I was running my sustainability products innovation project, I managed, through Unlocked, to get my hands on an employee who had worked on west African rural support projects, another who had spent 10 years at the leading edge of user experience (UX) design, a woman who had been seconded from a top consulting firm to the WEF for 3 years to summarise the current state of sustainable mobility incentivisation schemes, a guy who had spent 10 years working in a payments customer service centre, a sustainable ag scientist who'd run away from Monsanto and a post-blockchain distributed security geek. They were based in four continents and all had day jobs that had frustratingly little to do with sustainability as it happens. Once we overcame some of the time difference, linguistic and social disconnects, the team hummed. You don't start with DEI – you start with wanting to survive and thrive and then you recruit actively and intelligently (by looking beyond the cliched metrics). People recently have knowingly politicised DEI (rather than following dumbly along for the lolz). They are in some ways like people who disparage critiques of elites and the rapidly accelerating concentration of wealth against a backdrop of decades of flat real earnings as 'bringing politics into it' or 'encouraging class war'.

3 *Disruptive innovation is radical innovation.* Most innovation is to some extent disruptive. But most innovation, including radical innovation, is not disruptive innovation, properly understood. The major disruptive innovations are both more than radical and less. Put differently, they change smaller things with greater effect. Definitions vary but for our purposes we can agree that incremental innovation changes a product or other aspect of the business; radical innovation changes a whole business model; and disruptive innovation is one particular way to change an industry. Almost all actual innovation is type one or two, while almost all innovation discussion is about type three, presumably because disruption sounds cooler and justifies less taxation. Disruption usually starts with a very small, simple intervention that addresses needs that have been abandoned. For a full and clear explanation of disruptive innovation, it's worth going back to its defining authority, the brilliant Clayton Christiansen.[6]

If you are determined to try your hand at disruptive innovation or want to check whether there is an opportunity there before investing most of your time and energy in the richly rewarding areas of incremental innovation and beyond, there are an interesting and rewarding set of exercises to try. My favourite is called 'addressable market battleships' and this is how you play it. Create two mixed teams. By mixed I mean you should ensure that you have front line, service centre, logistics, UX, etc., in both teams. One team works up a set of market segments currently served by the product, service, division, go-to-market or whatever you are looking to disrupt. It should be both the sacred cow and the main cash-cow of your company or division. Or one of the primary raisons d'être of your charity or department or agency. It should be what pays your bills and what you're famous for. It could be something your most senior people did really well before they got promoted. Each segment has to be justified. You'll need adjudicators for this. Blue team designs the missiles. A partial hit is an underserved or partly served segment. A direct hit is an underserved segment which is larger than at least one of the served segments. A fatal hit is a completely unserved segment which is larger than two or three or more of the served segments. You'll need an adjudicator for this as well. But even well-adjucated sessions of this leads to huge arguments. Which is sort of the point. Play it for a morning with pairs of teams or play it discontinuously over a communication and collaboration application like Slack or Teams for a week or two. Just play.

4 *Innovation is an event or epiphany.* Innovation is actually an approach and a philosophy and a set of networks and patterns. Many have written and spoken on this but John Kao's approach is particularly accessible and engaging, especially when he illustrates his point using jazz piano.[7] My whole purpose in this and the previous chapter is to shake you up and get you ready for this approach. You need to change your whole way of thinking about the impossibility of the challenges involved and the limits of your abilities to be creative when put in the right small gang of revolutionaries with the right coffee and the right biscuits.

5 *Innovation happens in special places with strange furniture and special people.* I'm sure you've come across the special innovation 'labs' or 'hubs' or 'spaces' that large companies that have completely lost the ability to innovate build, often in a converted industrial building with some of the plumbing and wiring left exposed. Sometimes they will include hugely expensive tech

demo units which then require hugely expensive security protection. Then they put some games and brightly coloured, weirdly shaped furniture, perhaps some swings or swinging chairs, and children's snacks in them in case they will make their employees behave like start-up kids. As a way of wasting vast amounts of money without catalysing any innovation at all, this approach has a lot to offer.

It may seem strange to have to say this, but furniture and room design have little to do with people and their motivations. If the weather is warm, you might be better off convening your team in the park, a café with big benches, a steam ferry playing jazz on Stockholm harbour, whatever. I've never yet seen a foosball table make people think creatively or feel more playful. In fact, now that I think about it, I've never yet seen a foosball table being used and they have featured prominently in four out of my last five employers. Maybe because it would be like putting on a t-shirt saying 'I'm so lazy and/or unimportant I've got time to play foosball.' Alexandra Deschamps-Sonsino has written an excellent account of all the ways in which creative spaces might or might not encourage collaboration and creativity. She is fair but sceptical about both relevance and return on investment (ROI). 'It's also important that no matter what you do to your work environment, it cannot compensate for some major basic flaws. If there is a significant pay gap between white men and others in the business, for example, chances are the innovation potential of the business won't be reached. It's very hard to have great ideas when you're angry at basic workplace inequalities.'[8]

Many of the most interesting and successful approaches both in business and elsewhere are the result of networks and chains of users, advocates, etc. Try an exercise with your team where you identify who could become part of your innovation movement. Who will have their pain or frustration addressed? Who will have an unmet need met? Who will find it easier to do the things they have to do anyway? Who will be inspired to try something they never thought they could do before? Who will be inspired to be part of a group they thought wouldn't have them? Who will make money from this innovation apart from you? Who will see their identity confirmed, enabled, cherished or enhanced? Who will sing and dance when they hear about it? Or chuckle with pleasure? *Who will want to tell your story for you?* Empower your team to imagine and write down what it would be like to build a movement or a coalition, aligning the frustrated, the annoyed, the ignored and the motivated.[9]

Notes

1   Carlin, *Brain Droppings*, Hyperion, 1998.

2   Marketing Charts, 7 August 2017, https://www.marketing-charts.com/industries/retail-and-e-commerce-79421

3   Campbell, THJ, 1980.

4   It's well worth reading Steven Johnson's beautiful book, *Where Good Ideas Come From*, which highlights the progress of the 'slow hunch' through chains of innovation as well as the huge importance of collaborative clusters where the magic of seren-dipity can flourish. Johnson, WGICF, Riverhead, 2010. Also see some nicely presented recent research by Rocio Lorenzo at BCG, Munich. https://www.ted.com/talks/rocio_lorenzo_want_a_more_innovative_company_hire_more_women#t-299140

5   Cappelli & Tavis, TPMR, *HBR Magazine*, October 2016.

6   There is a great one-hour talk by him at Oxford. https://www.youtube.com/watch?v=rpkoCZ4vBSI

    A generous set of resources is shared at his own website: https://hbr.org/2020/01/the-essential-clayton-christensen-articles

7   Kao, IN, 2007 and his talks: https://johnkao.com

8   Deschamps-Sonsino, CCI, p. 114.

9   Charles Leadbeater is compelling on this and you will find links to all his books and some inspirational talks here: https://

charlesleadbeater.net/category/videos/ The fabulous Robin Chase, co-founder of Zipcar and radical thinker about collaboration platforms has long combined theory and practice based on this insight. See www.robinchase.org and Chase, PI, 2015.

It is also worth taking a deep dive into the experiences of the Mondragon cluster of cooperatives forming the Mondragon Corporation. https://www.mondragon-corporation.com/en/

Also see Leadbeater on learning from the edges and frugal innovation http://charlesleadbeater.net/2014/02/the-frugal-innovator/

See also Radju and Prabhu on frugal innovation. http://frugal-innovationhub.com/en/

And for some interesting developments in the corporate sector, various articles in HBR on reverse innovation: https://hbr.org/2012/04/a-reverse-innovation-playbook

chapter 3

Get your motivation right and you're halfway there

'You could attach prices to thoughts. Some cost a lot, some a little. And how does one pay for thought? The answer, I think, is with courage.'

Ludwig Wittgenstein[1]

It is my contention that the main driver of successful innovation is not just the effective real-world application of free will or intention, the breaking free from constricting imaginary determination of various kinds, but, curiously, a purpose focussed on giving more expression to the free will of others. This intention, this purpose is what drives a mission and without intelligently constructed mission-driven innovation we are headed for yet deeper troubles. The understanding of any language, whether linguistic, software or design, depends on and assumes free will. A physically caused and fully determined reaction cannot, by definition, ground meaning, value or beauty.[2] The purpose that drives successful innovation is always rooted in the respect for freedom, which is fundamental to humanity; further, the respect for free will which is distinctively human. A successful innovation nearly always identifies a frustrated choice, perhaps one that is not yet even known, a frustrated opportunity to be more human. Innovation through the solution of such frustrations becomes the instantiation of respect for free will and is thus the engine of human flourishing.

In a profound sense, innovators are people who have freed themselves from deterministic thinking. Free thinking, thinking rooted in a belief in and respect for free will, is by definition a rejection of deterministic thinking. Examples of deterministic thinking are many. It could be the materialistic determinism of later Marxism and its many subsequent offspring, which argues for the inescapable material determinants of many social and political events and decisions. Or perhaps it could be the inherent determinism of the type of neo-liberalism that lay behind the politics of Reagan and Thatcher and their spiritual children, which argues for the determining consequences of unfettered market forces. We were already surrounded but new determinisms are emerging from the spurious acceptance or defence of the inevitability of algorithms in social networking and search to the unthinking application of AI to automation, which are again being presented as givens without question. And there are many others including the dangerous return of eugenics[3] and thinly veiled defences of male and white supremacy,[4] often masquerading as scientifically proven and therefore inescapable.[5] Wherever we turn someone, generally for obscured reasons, perhaps even to themselves in many cases, is arguing that 'we have no choice'. There's nothing that the charlatan with an unjustifiable agenda loves more than a 'scientifically proven inevitability'. Nowhere is this more dangerously true today than in Putin's Russia, and Tim Snyder, History professor at Yale, has done deep work exposing the approach, the relationship between freedom, free will and determinism, and its consequences.[6] The true innovator doesn't accept this, not just intellectually but in their soul. Or as Peter Theil says, 'What important truth do very few people agree with you on'.[7]

Political philosopher, feminist and troublemaker, Lorna Finlayson has written passionately and persuasively about the more or less surreptitious ways that 'common sense' and 'generosity' police the interests of elites. This is true both in academic circles and in the political elites where political theory is vaguely understood but nonetheless influential. One of these relevant to us is the veiled determinism underpinning various uses of 'human nature' as in the sentence 'Idealists, dreamers, socialists and fools are admirable (in a childlike way) in their belief that human nature permits us to cooperate, behave generously, avoid greed and act in the best interests of our community.' This is a summary of a pervasive point of view you will be familiar with. For example, here is Boris Johnson talking to the Centre for Policy Studies in 2013: 'I don't believe that economic equality is possible; indeed some measure of inequality is essential for the spirit of envy and keeping up with the Joneses that is, like greed, a valuable spur to economic activity.' This is analogous to recent claims by Nigel Farage that he is allied with Andrew Tate because they both believe that criticising the 'natural' feelings of men has 'emasculated' them.[8] This is a view generally explicitly voiced in defence of extreme inequality and its handmaidens, perhaps most succinctly summarised by the great Keynesian, JK Galbraith, 'The modern conservative is engaged in one of man's oldest exercises in moral philosophy; that is, the search for a superior moral justification for selfishness.'[9] Finlayson compares it to victim blaming in rape cases in the sense that the greed, mendacity and selfishness we see on display in the political worlds are generally displayed by a tiny group who are benefitting hugely from the *inevitability* of this supposed human nature. But you don't need political philosophy to figure out what's going on here. Look at what happened during Covid. If your local community is anything like mine, the outpouring of fraternity, selflessness, volunteering and generosity was extraordinary. Shopping and caring for the old and vulnerable, supporting the extraordinary front line workers in nursing, delivery, food logistics and retail, and a hundred other unsung essential jobs. Various forms of communal solidarity and generosity accounted for the behaviour of 99 per cent of the population. Incomprehensibly to most, there remained a tiny sliver of politicians and entrepreneurs who woke up one day and said to themselves 'People are getting sick and dying in their thousands. The old and vulnerable seem particularly at risk. I smell an opportunity to set up a company selling faulty protective equipment and spend the excess profits on hiring private jets to go on holidays and buying yachts in the Med while paying only minimal donations and kickbacks (for now) to the chaps partying like it's the end of the world at 10 Downing Street.' Not only is this kind of behaviour not the norm, not 'the way people are', not 'human nature', it's so far beyond the norm that most people couldn't believe it was true until they saw the pictures.

Folk on the right politically have understood the fundamental importance of freedom and free will in their pursuit of the rights of individuals to freedom of choice, their 'freedom to' express, possess and behave. Those on the left have understood this fundamentally in their focus on the collective agreements we need to make to unlock individual freedom and flourishing, typically through a 'freedom from' poverty, ill health and ignorance.[10] Both sides typically underestimate the extent to which they take for granted the freedoms the other has fought for. At their worst, the left sacrifices all interest in innovation itself as a fetish of capitalism and the engine of unsustainable growth while apparently forgetting the huge increases in basic quality of life for all that it has brought. Just as at their worst, the right has neglected the role that social and public orientated innovations underpin everything they need to flourish, right down to security, infrastructure, property rights, both tangible and intellectual and the tight, expertly managed and dynamic regulation of their precious, powerful markets. As they say in South Africa, a bird only flies if it has two wings.

The right has tended therefore to celebrate the innovators who make our individual lives better, which we often find in the private sector. The left, however, has celebrated the innovators who make our collective lives and communities better, which we tend to find in the public and third sectors. There is a politics of innovation, of course. And political ideologies of various kinds have abused or taken narrow approaches to it. I'm not qualified to tackle this complex set of questions. But for our purposes these divisions don't matter because most of the deep patterns we need to know about to innovate successfully are common to all. Perhaps because they are always rooted in respect for free will, free choice and the fulfilment of human wants through a deep understanding of and respect for human needs. This is why the uncovering of a new freedom which is at the heart of innovation is often rooted in an explicit or implicit form of multi-dimensional ethnography, the oblique approach to uncovering hidden unfreedoms.

As will be clear already, the successful innovation team will be attempting to reconcile an endless series of slightly inconsistent problems, or rather an endless series of problems with slightly inconsistent available solutions, through a series of trade-offs between speed, cost, material limits, personnel limits, demand requirements, product/market fit, etc. Not all innovations need to be so radical as to leap from one demand curve to another, but probably all successful innovation efforts are embarked upon with at least that secret radical intent. This whole process done well is not innovation. It is just good design – which is a very good thing indeed.

A true innovation creates a new approach which is likely disruptive of the product or service, the organisation or the market. But let's dwell first on the additional element which makes great innovation teams distinctively successful. *Purpose* is rooted in a passionate interest in and deep understanding of the happiness and well-being of the customer or citizen – the prospective beneficiary of the innovation. It gives voice and focus to the desire to improve the world in some way. This is why innovation is so fundamental, so daunting, so hard and so important. It is part of the way by which we become more human by working with others to improve our environment, our tools and toys, our complete surroundings.

The driving purpose that gives a logic and coherence to the thousand trade-offs of design is a particular instantiation of the desire to increase joy and happiness of some group of people.

Adding shared purpose rooted in customer understanding to a diverse group of deeply skilled people is like throwing petrol on fire. Such a team has an unfair advantage over all other practitioners. Here is Bill Aulet, serial entrepreneur, MD of the Martin Trust centre for MIT Entrepreneurship and author of a great book on start-ups,[11] 'I used to think corporate culture didn't matter. Discussion of vision, mission and values was for people who couldn't build product or sell it! We had work to do and this MBA BS was getting in the way! And then my first company failed. Cambridge Decision Dynamics did not fail because we didn't have great technology or a great product or customers. It failed as a sustainable, scalable organisation because we had no meaningful purpose to create team unity to fight through the tough times.'[12]

If you have broad mission and customer obsession but no tightly focussed purpose, you are most likely a charity rather than an innovation group. If you have the skills and the mission but no deep customer understanding, you are most likely a government department or agency. And if you have the technical skills and deep customer understanding but no sense of shared purpose or mission, you're probably a bank or an average company, trading on past innovations. Perhaps in a death spiral too slow for a senior management blinded by weekly, monthly and quarterly targets to perceive. This tripartite analysis is trite, rude and simplistic. Yet strangely accurate.

We are daunted by the complexity of the inconsistencies and tensions we are working with. The inconsistencies of cost, time, material possibility. And the inconsistencies of approach and language and tools between our strategists, our engineers, our designers and ethnographers, our coders, policy makers, strategists and builders. We reach fearfully for systems and processes. Stop. The resolution of these tensions doesn't lie in processes. I know that is almost impossible for those educated in western business schools to comprehend. But it's true. Processes are just one of the tools we need to use. The resolution lies in purpose. A purpose rooted in an understanding of real human needs resolves all conflicts. This is innovation.

What kind of purpose? Let's look at some successful examples:

'To make the running shoes so cool you wouldn't want to run in them.'

'To build a cheap transit system that will get people on the edge of town to work in under half an hour.'

'To make air travel accessible to ordinary people.'

'To deliver good healthcare to all, regardless of wealth.'

'To organise the world's information and make it universally accessible.'

'To save people money so they can live better.'

'To give all children an education that will transform their opportunities.'

'To make washing dishes laughably easy.'

'To protect citizens from crime and the fear of crime.'

'To make it more valuable to keep a forest than to lose it.'

'To be free to go out and not miss the latest episode of *Gilligan's Island*.'

And here are some fabulously stupid ones:

'To set the highest possible standards as well as securing maximum market potential.'

'To create a shopping experience that pleases our customers; a workplace that creates opportunities and a great working environment for our associates; and a business that achieves financial success.'

'To shape the future of the Internet by creating unprecedented value and opportunity for our customers, employees, investors, and ecosystem partners.'

'To inspire and nurture the human spirit – one person, one cup, and one neighborhood at a time.'

'To be one of the world's great specialist banking groups, driven by commitment to our core philosophies and values.'[13]

It's a useful exercise and non-trivially difficult and time consuming to make your innovation group articulate a purpose like those on the first list.

Can devotion to my company or agency be my purpose? It is bizarre and surprising that so many otherwise apparently averagely intelligent managers and leaders still attempt to impose this dangerously perverted idea on their benighted staff. It's as if they have forgotten that it is only and simply by being devoted to their citizens or customers that they have a mandate to exist. That focussing on the missing needs of these people is what led them to exist in the first place, the engine of all innovation, which in turn is the engine of all enterprise.

Some senior leaders even refer to the company being 'a family'. If your leader keeps referring to your company as a family, be very afraid.[14] (Unless it actually is a family.) For a start, most families don't fire people. And organisations that don't fire people die. (This is one of the many reasons that most charities and government administrations are in such terrible shape – the former think it's mean to fire people, rather than realising it's often far meaner to everyone else not to. While the latter just aren't allowed to for good but not good enough reasons.) It also implies you shouldn't feel too bad about giving your evenings and weekends to your employer.

The great company, just like the great public or third-sector organisation, believes above all else in making the lives of its customers or citizens better. Governments and charities want to do this by definition – their purpose is written on the tin, even if they seem sometimes to have trouble reading their own tins. Companies are very different from governments in several ways; on the downside, if they don't innovate, they die but, on the upside, they only have to serve who they want to serve – pesky overly demanding or unprofitable customers and the poor can be turned away, a luxury unavailable to democratically accountable governments, at least in theory. But in this one fundamental respect they are the same – every great company and every government department and agency and every charity started by having *a burning desire to solve a particular problem for a particular group of people.*

It needn't be a big problem. Listen to the group of innovators who founded TiVo, a digital set-top box that allowed scheduled recording, pausing and rewinding, which arguably started a revolution that completely disrupted the way we think about home entertainment:

'Howard Look: I came on in early 1998 . . . I was a video junkie. My wife and I, we watched a lot of TV. My job was to program the VCR in the morning every day before work. We had seven VHS tapes for Saturday through Sunday, which I would program . . .

Richard Bullwinkle (TiVo's chief evangelist, 1998–2002): People didn't realize the need – that you should never have to stay home to watch Friends. But NBC had us brainwashed . . . Howard Look: I put it in my wife's hand. We called it "waf," or "wife acceptance factor." We wanted this to be a different consumer product, not just for the typical nerdy guy bringing something new home from Best Buy so the wife would say, "We don't need another remote." Mike Ramsay: I think Howard had the idea of using the remote to vote on something you like or don't like. We wanted to get TiVo biased to knowing your preferences. We used a thumb up and thumb down.

Howard Look: I remember watching Siskel and Ebert and thinking, "That's how people think about TV shows, too."'[15]

There you have it in a few words. You should never have to stay home to watch *Friends*. You shouldn't need a doctorate to programme your VCR. Your preferences should be remembered. And the interface should be simple and beautiful. These customer joy obsessed weirdos innovated the Netflix generation.

And here's designer Ben Terret who worked with Mike Bracken and Tom Loosemore on the first iterations of gov.uk:

> **'The design challenge here seems to be – don't avoid the obvious. Government websites are needs driven and what people want to do is get in, get what they want and then get out. Quickly.'**[16]

So simple to say, yet so complex and hard and impactful to achieve. Some people belittle the early website-focussed achievements of gov. uk as 'just a website' but it changed the relationship between the government and citizens of the UK in a million small ways, a million small problems solved, an aspiration beautifully summarised by Christian Bason as: 'Every contact between a citizen and their government is a moment of truth'.[17] And that excellent team and its successors went on to create several more profound and complex innovations like 'Verify', the first and only robust national online identity verification system that had transformational implications that go far beyond the admittedly profound impact it could have on citizen–government relationships, before the tax department, HMRC killed it for parochial power reasons. We will look at how to prevent that kind of death, or at least mitigate the risk of it, in Chapter 7 on Adoption.

And here is an extract from the Apple Lisa design manifesto shortly after Steve Jobs and his team visited Xerox parc twice in 1979:

> **'Lisa must be fun to use. It will not be a system that is used by someone "because it is part of the job" or "because the boss told them to." Special attention must be paid to the friendliness of the user interaction and the subtleties that make using the Lisa rewarding and job-enriching.'**[18]

The Lisa project failed in commercial terms, but we know exactly where an almost maniacal devotion to this philosophy led in the end. Here is Apple designer/coder, Ken Kocienda, commenting on exactly the same philosophy 39 years later.

> '[S]o it was logical that our attention to creating designs that work looped back around to inform our refined-like responses, the way we tried to find balance, and our effort to create a pleasing and integrated whole. The added benefit is that this entire cycle removed arbitrariness from taste. *It gave taste a purpose,* a rationale beyond self-indulgence, an empathetic end.' [19][my emphasis]

That sense of purpose is literally what drove these innovations. Once a company loses sight of this, as they generally do, they are in the early stages of death or the advanced stages of corruption through oligopoly and regulatory capture.

How can you tell if a company is in this stage? If it's making acquisitions to make up for the fact that it's too big and slow to innovate any more, that is fine, and all is good. Nothing wrong with using your cash to compensate for your lack of agility, creativity and originality. And if you want to spend a bit of money on pointless internal innovation divisions or labs that nobody listens to – for marketing and dignity purposes – that's fine too. Most large companies can't even begin to innovate – or rather they can begin but the corporate antibodies kill most good ideas before they get much beyond prototype stage. So, they go out and buy beautiful minnows. Which is sensible.

A company that has turned its back on both acquisitions and deep R&D is in trouble. If it's doing share buy-backs, it is clearly no longer in the business of innovating to delight. It is in the business of legal market manipulation to increase the value of the holdings of the equity holders. And particularly those very special equity holders who are managing the company and making the decision to buy back shares. A company that literally can't think of a better use for its surplus cash or borrowing power than buying its own shares to inflate the holdings of the senior executives has tragically lost the will to innovate and will soon be gone from the face of God's green earth. The deep digging done by Professor William Lazonick at the University of Massachusetts has highlighted both the unbelievable scale and various potentially economically damaging consequences of this practice, but for our purposes it is the signal it sends about the innovation intent of the firm and the cumulative impact it has on innovation and thus productivity that is of profound concern.[20]

There are those who might object that there is surely no good purpose driving the banks or the oil companies. I think that's probably misguided. Both sectors started life and continued for many decades as deeply innovation-driven clusters of companies that aspired to and succeeded in transforming our wellbeing for the better. Both lie at the very heart of much of our economic growth over the last two centuries and achieved it through countless impressive innovations.

Dwell for a moment on the extraordinary feats of creativity that have resulted in the global system for extracting, refining and distributing oil from the 1500 main fields to the billions of end points where it fuels our various habitable systems. The fact that we must now turn away fast from carbon-intensive economies is not their fault – although it might have been nice if some of them hadn't decided to systematically fund deliberate ignorance in defence of their increasingly deadly incumbency. Now we need a similar set of networked innovations to create a global system of renewable energy supplies at scale and pace. This may be a job for governments to drive, just as they drove most of the work to build the infrastructure underpinning the oil industry. Companies and industries will attempt to outstay their welcome by their very nature. We shouldn't expect them to commit commercial suicide. Caring about planetary carrying capacity is clearly not part of their core competencies.

The case of financial services, and the banking sector in particular, is more complex. Financial services were established to innovate in the area of pricing, managing and sharing risk. But the rewards returning to innovation in regulatory arbitrage, regulatory evasion and financial engineering for profit maximisation in the short term led to them taking a different set of risks, safe in the knowledge that their systemic centrality would ensure tax payer socialisation of the downside of their risks, long after the offshore privatisation of its upside had disappeared into the ether.[21]

I'm not arguing that you have to have a *good* purpose to achieve innovation. It's obvious that there have been evil innovations. I'm arguing that virtually all successful innovation is motivated by a desire to improve the world and the free choices of the people in it. Likewise, unregulated monopoly, financialisation and radically rising inequality have now led to a slowing of innovation in the USA over the last 20 years. The risks we face from power law accelerations of networked risk can only be met by power law accelerations of networked innovation. I have dwelled on some of the systemic barriers to innovation because it is not a given that it will outpace the catastrophic risks we face from climate, AI, pandemics, populism and the intertwined forces of plutocracy and kleptocracy, the capture and corruption of government policy-making by the rich, of the rich, for the rich.

While considering *good* purposes for driving innovation it may be worth pondering a minute on that late twentieth-century aberration, Corporate Social Responsibility and its various offspring, ESG (Environmental, Social and Governance) and so on. So first let's get straight what the sectors do. The private sector exists and thrives to the extent that it creates solutions to what specific groups of people want or need and are prepared to pay for. The public and third sectors exist, among other things, to solve wicked problems and failures of the commons, to manage systemic challenges by pooling risk and averting catastrophe for the few by sharing burdens across the many, to give expression to shared identity through solidarity with the poor, the sick, the young and the old, to create shared security and protection of intellectual and material property and to regulate markets.

The private sector looks on at all this complex goodness with a good deal of envy. Marketing departments think that if they could give the appearance of helping poor people and children, it would be great for their brands. But they have forgotten why they existed in the first place, *to innovate to meet the needs of particular groups of people*. And they have lost sight of the fact that this is a deeply noble cause that has brought great joy and ease and happiness to billions. It is *good enough*. Trumpeting random acts of kindness is no substitute for the fact that you've lost the art of innovating new causes of happiness, the core of your purpose. The marketing win is short term, but the damage endures.

You might also have the misfortune to hear that a company has the intention of 'doing well by doing good'. If you do, check you still have your wallet and head for the nearest exit. They will have very selective amnesia when it comes to what doing good means. Generally, you will find that it means, among other things, pandering to autocrats and quasi-fascist dictators on a daily basis. Bear in mind that a fully functioning monarchy is just a dictatorship with a good marketing department. It is right that companies deal with these countries – until governments tell them not to. It's not up to companies to decide who is good and bad – they aren't qualified or equipped. So they should just shut up about doing good unless they mean meeting unmet demands through innovation, production and distribution. That's doing good by doing well.

Companies do of course have social responsibilities already:

To treat their staff well and pay them properly.

To treat them fairly and equitably regardless of their gender, race, sexuality or age.

To create working environments where it is literally unthinkable that senior people in general (and men in particular) make junior people in general (and women in particular) feel unsafe, humiliated, exploited, blackmailed or objectified.

To obey the laws of the countries they operate in, including the environmental laws; the transparency and accounting laws; and the tax laws.

To try to avoid creating damage and deficit in the world.

To recognise and manage their negative externalities and, where level regulatory playing fields are required to achieve that, make common cause with their competitors in good faith to help their governments create and safeguard them.

To avoid monopolies and oligopolies.

To stop paying bribes.

To demand the same standards of their supply chains.[22]

And to innovate to make the world a better place.

If they've really done all those things and they still hanker to do even more good in the world, they should check again whether they've paid their taxes and then pay their workers more.

It's not complex. It might be hard but it's not complex.

If a company is making acquisitions, not to compensate for losing the art of innovation, but to move towards or defend a quasi-monopolistic position, it will find itself in trouble before long. The gods created companies to delight people on earth and the companies that delight are beloved. A monopoly is a strategy to make people use you, not because you are beloved, but because they have no frickin' choice. This was well identified by Schumpeter. Schumpeter saw two main threats to the flourishing of capitalism and the consequent growth of economies; a form of intellectual socialism, by education, experience and taste ignorant of business in every way, that would seek to destroy free enterprise and private property through creeping corporatism. And a form of advanced statist monopolisation and regulatory capture as businesses sought to prevent the threat posed by entrepreneurialism of a never-ending threat of creative destruction by cosying up to the state and colluding with it in the creation of barriers to entry in the guise of regulation. History has been kind to both predictions.

This is not wholly dissimilar to the argument of wildly successful entrepreneur Peter Theil, whose excellent book *Zero to One*[23] advocates early pursuit of monopoly positions as a deliberate strategy for start-ups. But this is the natural temporary monopoly that flows from the uniqueness that is a definitional side effect of innovation. Every successful innovator is a temporary monopolist. The monopoly that flows from innovation and may be preserved for as long as possible is beneficial to creation. But as Theil, no socialist, himself acknowledges: 'To an economist, every monopoly looks the same, whether it deviously eliminates rivals, secures a license from the state, or innovates its way to the top. In this book we're not interested in illegal bullies or government favorites: by "monopoly", we mean the kind of company that's so good at what it does that no other firm can offer a close substitute.'[24]

The monopoly that is sought through collusive barriers to entry after innovation dies is a very different thing from the uniqueness that follows innovation and is its prize. It is interesting to wonder whether, if our economists had a little more understanding of business and the role of innovation in it, they would have studied the dynamics of positive and negative monopolisation more closely and we would now be in a better position to regulate the emerging incumbent platforms like Google, Netflix, Facebook and Amazon before they wreak even more social damage than they already have.[25] Disguising the monopolies created by platform and network effects with non-monopolies in market adjacencies doesn't really address the problem. We need to look no further than the way Amazon treats its employees, suppliers and competitors and Facebook treats its customer data and electoral manipulation and all of them treat their tax obligations to see the consequences of forgetting to regulate monopoly. An increasing and understandable desire to retreat to cash and other analogue systems may be one interesting consequence. Cash is to cards as vinyl is to Spotify.

The move from incumbency to oligopoly and then monopoly seems attractive because the alternative is usually certain death. What makes the corrupting nature of monopoly analogous to the corrupting nature of autocracy and dictatorship is their shared denial of choice. The denial of consumer choices is the less deadly analogue of the denial of citizen choice. A monopoly, like an autocracy or dictatorship, needs to worry less about the choices its customers can't make. And it's unlikely to be an accident that we see increasingly close collaboration between monopolists and autocrats. The fire that drives innovation is the understanding of the importance of this in any sector. Innovation is lit by a love of free choice and a desire to serve it, whether with running shoes too cool to run in or a health system free at the point of need. The alternative to innovation is the descent from stagnation, by way of incumbency, oligopoly and monopoly to corruption and kleptocracy. This is why we need innovation in politics, political parties and political institutions as well, although it seems from my limited experience that political parties know even less about innovation than large corporations and government departments.

As always when seeking to innovate, it might be useful to identify and uproot the effects of binaries by the application, in the first instance of a trinary analysis. This uncommon intellectual manoeuvre frees us from the determinism of the either/or, which is still implicit in the consultant's favourite substitute for fresh thinking – the two by two. Here's a simple practical exercise you can try in your workplace. If you see a consultants' two-by-two analysis of your strategic options, print it out and then tear it in half. Place the two halves together and tear them in half again so that you have four pieces. Put these four pieces in the bin and begin thinking.

For example, if we wanted to break down the binary of equality/inequality we could introduce the third element of fraternity or liberty. What we can't allow in a trinary analysis are non-excluding false choices like equality or liberty; the trinary element allows us to envision liberty with equality and with inequality and everywhere in between, highlighting which positions are impossible and mapping different polities and polices. Dwell on this for a minute because it is very interesting for anyone embarking on political or policy innovation. As soon as you're trapped into thinking that the opposite of inequality is equality you are sunk – because it's easy to prove that the pure straw woman of equality is both impossible and scary. The opposite of inequality is fraternity. As soon as we acknowledge our common and interdependent humanity, we begin to see how damaging inequalities are, not only to individual dignity, but to the viability and sustainability of our communities and nations.

Once we abandon binaries we think more in terms of common principles and the way they inform directions of travel rather than tribes and arrival points. A related false dichotomy is the one between equality and liberty on which most left/right politics is founded. Fraternity dissolves it and allows you to pursue both – in constant tension with each other. It's not a perfect approach but as an alternative to monarchy it's a social innovation that has proven fruitful.

You only need to spend a little time contemplating the extraordinary and positive disruptions being pioneered by the trans and gender non-conforming movements to realise that stepping away from the constraints of gender and sexuality binaries opens galaxies of innovative possibility almost too wonderful to contemplate. You might think it odd or even outrageous to innovate with gender, sexuality and the forms that loving human relationships can take, but this is how people felt about suggesting that a plenitude of new insights and discoveries might derive from questioning whether the sun revolved around the earth. And I'm not taking a position here on what is biologically or in other ways physically determined. There is no return to disruptive innovation from denying physics or biology. But the possibly infinite recombination and interpretation of the underlying makeup of the world and the humans in it are endlessly fertile ground for the would-be innovator.

The particular trinary I have in mind to crystallise these thoughts in the business sector is the key investment and innovation analytic of rule taker, rule breaker, rule maker, first popularised, as far as I know, by David Gardner at The Motley Fool investment site/book/podcast/etc. Many firms have traditionally been locked in the false binary of whether to be a rule taker or a rule breaker. Few are given the possibility, wisdom or serendipity to be rule makers, but it tends toward being a licence to print money if you can find a way to do it. (Just to be clear, it's the 'rules' of the industry or market we are talking about here, not the rules of the regulators and state.) In the diagram below, the larger triangle represents the simplified field of business possibility. It is relatively easy to position different firms on this field or, more interestingly, track the progress of a single firm over time. The smaller triangle represents the field of effective policy, highlighting the public good flaws with the extreme of each position.

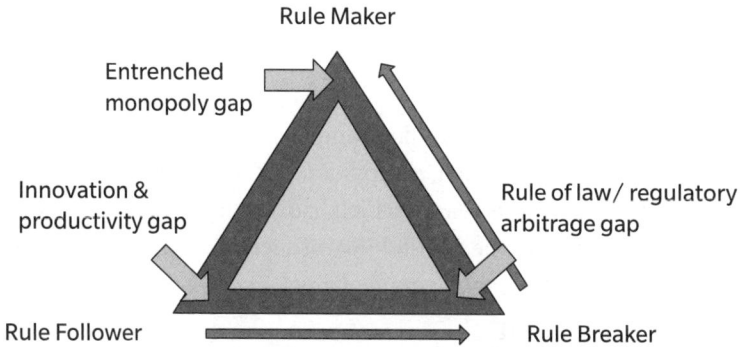

Rule followers are a joy for policy makers and regulators until slowly but surely they realise that the lack of innovation intrinsic to that position challenges productivity and the resultant economic growth with a series of increasingly challenging consequences in terms of the affordability of pensions, healthcare, defence and so on. By contrast, rule markers are an absolute boon to innovation, productivity and growth but are likely to leverage their excessive profits to entrench their market positions with a view to turning the inevitable temporary monopoly that radical and disruptive innovation gifts to the entrepreneur into a semi-permanent one. This ultimately results in rent seeking, price gouging and other market abuses ultimately devastating for the very productivity and growth they were originally prized for. The wise government seeks to push their wealth-generating industries towards the always unstable third position of tolerated rule breaking – up to a point. Too much political lobbying power for either labour or capital leads to stagnating growth and social disaster. At the moment we are deep into the latter threat and it's not even clear if or how we can find a way back.

Having cleared away a number of misunderstandings and obstacles as well as furnishing ourselves with some valuable tools, we are ready to roll up our sleeves and get to work, starting with that elusive but essential first step, creativity.

Notes

1   Wittgenstein, LCV, p. 52.

2   See Annex B for some explanation.

3   Nelson, TRE, 2016.

4   Klein, SHCMARS, 2018.

5   The most striking and ironic example, given his repeated attacks on neo-Marxism, is provided by the bizarre pseudo-science of Jordan Petersen, in which badly bungled biology is conscripted to justify the inevitability of social hierarchies. For one excellent account among many: Oliver, Scott, TFEOJP, 2018.

6   Snyder, TRTU, 2018.

7   Theil, ZTO, 2014.

8   *The Guardian*, 3 July 2024.

9   Galbraith, 1964.

10 Famously laid out in Isiah Berlin's classic *Two Concepts of Liberty*, OUP 1969 and recently beautifully explored for its relevance to the crisis we face right now, particularly in western democracy with the renaissance of fascism by Tim Snyder in *On Freedom*, Penguin, 2024.

11 DE, updated, 2024.

12 Aulet, CESB, 2014.

13 The first five people to send me the correct attribution for all 16 of these will win five free copies of this book to give to their favourite enemies.

14 Apart from the brilliant box set *Silicon Valley*. The best account of this and the many other strange perversities of Silicon Valley management is *Uncanny Valley* by Anna Weiner.

15 Roston, TTIWBM, 2019. [https://onezero.medium.com/they-thought-it-was-black-magic-an-oral-history-of-tivo-7503d0a-da8e0]

16 https://gds.blog.gov.uk/2012/01/19/designing-govuk/

17 Bason, LPSI, p. xx.

18 Hiltzik, DOL, p. 343.

19 Kocienda, IADP, p. 188.

20 Lazonick, PWP, *HBR* September 2014. For a counterargument
    that the rise in buybacks merely represents a reasonably pro-
    ductivity neutral rebalancing between dividends and buybacks
    following the 1982 change in legislation, see Koller, Tim,
    ASBJFG, 2015. Also see the various papers by the not-for-profit
    FCLT.org 'Focusing Capital on the Long Term began in 2013 as
    an initiative of the Canada Pension Plan Investment Board and
    McKinsey & Company, which together with BlackRock, The
    Dow Chemical Company, and Tata Sons founded FCLTGlobal in
    July 2016.'

21 Mulgan, TLAB, p. 25, 2013.

22 Although this needs to be done with care as it is often used to
    exclude new entries to a market.

23 Theil, ZTO, 2014.

24 Theil, ZTO, p. 24

25 Galloway, TF, 2017.

chapter 4

Post-it notes aren't enough – the creativity challenge

'I'm a bit crazy so sometimes I get these mad ideas that on paper aren't even possible. But in my head I think "Yeah, fuck it, let's do it".'[1]

Stormzy

At the heart of the activity that constitutes the first stage of innovation is the elusive concept of the breakthrough idea, the much-celebrated eureka moment. In myth and self-marketing this is the only important point that is perpetually refined, retailed and revered as if magic lies there and everything else is secondary. We shouldn't trouble ourselves too much with those myths. They risk alienating us from this important activity as if only wizards, geniuses or the serendipitously blessed are allowed to play.

Much has been written about the hacks, games and processes one might use with a group to squeeze a good idea out of them. Most of them seem to involve putting a huge number of Post-it notes on a vertical surface. Or multi-coloured Post-it notes where design thinking is implicated. Ironically, the man who claims to have invented the Post-it note, Alan Amron, has been pitching his eureka moment against 3M's in the courts for decades now. In his version, he was wanting to leave a note for his wife where she would see it and he stuck a piece of paper to the fridge with chewing gum and then presumably thought 'Wow I could turn that into a world-famous brainstorming product.' 3M's version uses the old trope of the failed experiment (in making glue) but with the folksy twist of a guy called Art Fry who used the rejected prototype to anchor his hymn book bookmark and was presumably singing the words of 'Come to us, creative Spirit, in this holy house; ev'ry human talent hallow, hidden skills arouse' by David Mowbray[2] and thought 'Wow I could turn this sticky failed prototype into a world-famous brainstorming product.'[3] Well clearly someone's lying about the origins of the Post-it note and from what we know about innovation, it could be both. But there's something fabulously ironic about the fact that this confusion lies at the origin of the damn thing because all those processes that use Post-it notes are a bit of a lie too. Believe it or not, you can't make difficult, complex, design-led thinking that much easier by using Post-it notes. It's a bit like the contribution of a pedometer to training for a marathon, a small useful technical addition that still leaves all the hard work to be done.

And yet, despite all the bullshit talked about this, there is still something special there that needs to happen. All the other strategies I discuss here will help you uncover it, will perhaps make it more likely and will lead you to the door of really good break-through ideas and creative solutions. And the hacks and games will help too. And maybe, sometimes, in the right hands, the Post-it notes. But what is it that allows some people to step through that door? What is the magic ingredient in coming up with a really great idea? Because although this eureka concept is way overplayed and mythologised, that may be for a good reason. I think there is some-thing magical about that moment, something ineffably human and exciting. And it may even be that some people are naturally more gifted at it, although we can all do things to become more prepared.

When people say 'There's no mystery about innovation – it's a skill that can be learned like any other' I want to say 'Yes, well I know what you mean. There is an awful lot to learn but . . . '. But what? What happens when you have created the right conditions and have the right unifying purpose and your minds are prepared to uncover the relevant breakthrough? That spark of originality and creativity is common to many human endeavours. You could perhaps teach someone everything Itzhak Perlman knew about playing the violin, but they won't create those moments that take off into the sublime, as Perlman can. There is something of the child-like in that moment of freedom, something playful and also something *fearless*. It's true that you probably must be unafraid of the truly new, to question or reject the commonly accepted given, the 'common sense' of inevi-tability. And as I've already said several times, that is the moment of freedom, the exercise of free will, the tiny inexplicable hemmed around but ultimately undetermined spark. And although everyone has free will, not everyone can use it to light a fire in that particular way.

It's also dependent on this combination of discipline, approach and preparation, which is all hard, time-consuming work without any shortcuts, with the ability to ask the right question at the right time and be free to come up with the unobvious answer, the strange answer, the new answer. Peter Theil makes a good case for the form of that question being 'What important truth do very few people agree with you on?' But I think that over-indexes on one of the paths the questioning mind can follow. Many of the design techniques that practitioners have popularised set the stage for more nuanced versions of this question, or rather the question 'How will you uncover an important truth that people have not yet understood?' This allows us to sort through the various hacks and techniques available and uncover the pattern language at play here. I think there are about four basic patterns to make a strong start with, but you could definitely make the case for more if you felt like it.

What are the sources of pain for our customers/citizens? What could be a cause for unexpected joy?

It's important to understand that focus groups with customers or citizens don't really help to uncover these truths. Most people misunderstand the causes of their pain and mis-identify the potential sources of their future joy. A far more intelligent ethnography is required, often walking with people through the complex chains of events they deal with or observing them if that's possible and recreating them as authentically as possible if they're not. But this alone won't lead to innovation. It may trigger it or prepare the ground for it, and it is certainly essential in many cases. But you could study horse and buggy users until the cows come home without thinking of a car. When the Xerox PARC team demonstrated their developments to Xerox senior management in 1977, the executives couldn't grasp the incredible significance of what they were looking at because none of them used office systems. The concept of personal computing didn't exist yet. PARC had invented it.

I can still remember that generation of managers who ordered PCs for their desks to make them look modern but they had to get their PAs to turn them on and get something impressively analytical displayed on the screen, a pie chart for example. These were the same PAs who had to print out emails, highlight them with marker pens and put them in a carboard folder with little fluorescent orientation tags attached. It's fascinating to note that after that fateful moment in the history of the information revolution, it was the wives of the Xerox executives who came up afterwards and asked to take a closer look. Because many of them were or had been secretaries. More on this beautiful story below.

An important term in this approach is 'source'. One of the mistakes innovation-seeking teams make repeatedly is to misunderstand the actual cause of the problem they are trying to solve, and many excellent design exercises and hacks seek to specifically address this trap. Large organisations exacerbate this problem to an often-fatal degree through both organisational and incentives structures. If I'm organisationally permitted or incentivised to think about a particular product, service, approach or modality, that's what I will do. Colloquially speaking, all problems look like nails if you work in Metal Tools Division and your bonus depends on how much you dress, think and behave like a hammer.

Governments have a particular problem with this challenge because of the complexity of their challenges and the divided nature of their governance. If you are trying to reduce reoffending in the criminal justice system, you may be needing to think about training, housing, through the gate mentoring, tax incentives, transport, media tropes and hidden agendas and a dozen other factors. Or if your Health Minister has asked you to innovate around reductions in childhood obesity, you better have permission to be thinking about urban design, transport systems, the location and pricing strategies of unprocessed food retailers, schools including curricula and teacher training, food industry structures and incentives, rural subsidies, social media, the advertising industry, GP surgeries and medical training, parental incomes, tax, welfare system effects and so on. Policy wonks and design consultants, even with unlimited Post-it notes, aren't going to cut it. You're going to need a rich diversity of experiences and ways of looking at the world in the room when you endeavour to reconstruct the sources of pain and frustration.

One of the ways in which design-led thinking subverts failed approaches in this area is because they are not analytical in the way that most companies and governments are structured to be. We have become increasingly damaged by our fearful reliance on consultants and experts who offer arcane silver bullets that just about never work. A simple but highly effective rule of thumb here is 'Never let an economist work unsupervised on a problem.' And you can substitute 'person with an MBA', 'self-important ivy league grad' and a number of other things for 'economist' in this sentence. Analysis is a beautiful thing in its place if you are asking the right unbiased questions and managing the analyst rigorously, but it risks the threat, like some consultancy, that it will provide impressive quasi-scientific justifications for decisions that somebody has already made or wants to make.

Christian Bason gives a nice clear exposition of the relationships between analysis and creativity and the associated relationships between service designers and lawyers, economists, etc.[4] The nudge trend, based on the work of Kahneman and other behavioural economists, risks substituting one bleak and reductive set of assumptions about human decision making for the clearly flawed rational economic decision-maker *homo economicus* theory that predated it. It's an improvement that policy innovators can't ignore, but we shouldn't think that most of the hard work of iterative, collaborative citizen-centred policy innovation can be avoided just because we have a little nudge unit of underqualified, inexperienced, young, white, middle-class arts graduates presenting simplistic bullshit on beautiful PowerPoints.[5]

Combining nudge with political cultures increasingly taking a policy-based evidence approach rather than the evidence-based policy making we originally aspired to can be literally deadly. A stark recent example is provided by the UK's approach to managing the SARS COV-2 pandemic in the early months of 2020. An over-reaching privatised consultancy with all the wrong incentives advocated for delaying lockdown on what appears to have been a largely spurious theory of 'behavioural fatigue'. This played well with Prime Minister Johnson, whose signature combination of arrogance, inattention to detail, intellectual mundanity and political laissez faire[6] on all interventions unlikely to profit his mates made him a willing co-conspirator with genuinely tragic consequences. Work by academics at Kings

College, London, has unpicked some of the causes of this failure.[7]
Sonia Sodha, herself arguably subject to tragically dangerous biases
in other areas of reporting, nailed the problem early and accurately:

> 'The problem with all forms of expertise in public policy is
> that it is often the most formidable salespeople who claim
> greater certainty than the evidence allows who are invited
> to jet around the world advising governments. But the
> irony for behavioural scientists is that this is a product of
> them trading off, and falling prey to, the very biases they
> have made their names calling out.
>
> I can only imagine how easy it might have been for
> Johnson to succumb to confirmation bias in looking for
> reasons to delay a lockdown: what prime minister wants
> to shut down the economy? And it is the optimism bias of
> the behavioural tsars that has led them to place too much
> stock in their own judgment in a world of limited evidence.
> But this isn't some experiment in a university psychology
> department – it is a pandemic and lives are at stake.'[8]

The converse case can be seen in many corporates where the fate
of beautifully structured and even creative innovation teams will
repeatedly have their disruptive and initially profit-diluting prototypes killed in the cradle by more senior executives who are optimising for personal three-year remuneration horizons rather than the
survivability of the firm. Which is why we need start-ups more than
ever as firms collude with governments to create ever larger barriers
to market entry. ESG has been an ironic gift to this poisonous trend
and Davos an accelerant.

To be productively creative, you will want to have experienced
customer-facing or service-centre staff in any innovation team
looking at products and services. There are few substitutes for
the wisdom of a seasoned front-line worker. And if you can't lay
the groundwork by doing *ethnographies of frustration*, consider
whether you find out about or tap into user workarounds. One of
the most celebrated case studies in this area is the Marin county

dudes who modified Schwinn clunkers for their races down Mount Tamalpais and the surrounding publicly accessible forest paths in the 60s: stiffer frames, modified gearing, wider tyres and ultimately huge suspension add-ons that gave a gravelly birth to the mountain bike industry, now worth about $12bn and on a CAGR (compound annual growth rate) path that could double that in the next 5 years. But there are many less obvious examples. Think of any badly designed park you've seen where the path takes one course and the people take another, even despite barriers, leaving well-worn evidence of the lack of customer focus indulged in by its original civic designers. Some corporate hotel chains have even started to put power points where you can access them on the desktop instead of forcing tired executives to crawl under their hotel room desks as if performing some obscure ritual obeisance to the gods of bad hotel design.

How do I do ethnographies of Frustration, and if I can't do that, what are my other practical alternatives? What follows below are some patterns you can apply in the creativity stage. I worked for a few years at the Young Foundation which pioneered this approach, rooted in Michael Young's work in the housing estates of East London and increasingly diversifying into digital and other cultural ethnographies leveraging the work of consumer ethnographers. But it is famously characteristic of ethnography that it is conducted by the white, privileged, educated upper classes on the groups who are none of these things. Its origins lie in colonialism as early anthropologists studied, through extended periods of co-habitation, the cultures of the colonised. Even by Michael Young's time, half a century after the pioneering work of Bronislaw Malinowski, when the strangers in our midst had become a valid subject of study, it was still a case of one class carefully and sympathetically examining another at close quarters. Alice Goffman's powerful and sympathetic urban ethnography of poor black men and their catastrophic policing in Chicago[9] has been deeply criticised for similar reasons. A far more powerful and promising approach is to work with insiders. At the Young Foundation we had the privilege of working with an extraordinary pioneer of this approach, the sociologist and ethnographer

Lisa McKenzie. Her first book, *Getting By*,[10] is a quintessential example of the ethnography of frustration, drawing on methodologies as diverse as Bourdieu's uncovering of habitus, Young's work in East London and Bev Skeggs' pioneering longitudinal ethnographies of women's experience of class and cognitive oppression. If you've ever wondered why the bizarre Illuminati family of conspiracy theories is still so prevalent, why people take drugs, why someone would spend a large piece of their weekly income on designer shoes or sunglasses, where people find strength, dignity, self-respect and courage in the face of unimaginable discrimination, disregard and disempowerment, you couldn't do better than read this and McKenzie's later lockdown diaries.

What is Nirvana? What would a more perfect future world look like in our neck of the woods?

We kicked off one of our more successful ideations offsites once by imagining that our CEO would be awarded the Nobel peace prize 10 years hence and then asking what would have had to happen just before that and so on back to the present. Working backwards from perfection is a beautiful provocation to creative thinking. I'm sad to say that none of the five projects that came from that offsite resulted in anyone getting a Nobel prize although one of them did make the front page of the *New York Times* and was chosen as one of *Time* magazine's 50 best inventions of 2009. And some of the other projects were extraordinary too. There are many similar such exercises. The essence of them is to approach your constrained thinking from a different angle, freed of the immovable objects and barriers you are so deeply familiar with that you can't think past them or around them, partly because you are so close to them that you can't see them. Every such exercise is, yet again, an attempt to think beyond inevitability.

The analogue of working to uncover the real causes of unhappiness in the previous section is working to understand the real barriers to improvement and breakthrough and your obscured assumptions about those barriers in this one. And having a manager at the front of the room saying, 'Assume makes an Ass out of U and me' isn't going to do the trick.

The point of these exercises is not to see who can come up with the craziest utopia; it's to cast the imaginative light of the participants on their assumptions from another direction. If we're going to build an electric car with a range of over 100 miles, then we're going to have to do some hard work rethinking battery life, charging infrastructures and the like. We end up innovating so much on storage that we won't be able to tell whether we're in the sustainable personal transport business or the home energy business. Or both. If we want to load metal containers straight from our trucks onto boats, we are going to have to find a whole new crane design partner. And a whole new metal box designer. And we're going to need a bigger boat. . .

Again, this line of thinking relieves us of the strictures of analysts and experts, at least for a while. We need to dream like children dream. And then we can ambush entrenched expertise from a fresh angle. Imagine you're trying to solve the problem of income inequality and you look ahead and see automation and AI sweeping a few million more jobs the way of manufacturing. You start by imagining a future where everyone gets a basic income that meets all basic needs: you can call it a universal basic income or a Freedom Dividend or whatever you like. You paint a rosy picture of human respect and flourishing, reengagement with communities and volunteering, and lifelong learning and so forth. It is only really when you've fallen in love with a possible future that you will have the will and the motivation to do the hard graft of examining the Alaskan, Finnish, Canadian and other basic income pilots to find out where the problems lie. And get serious analysts to see what the offsetting savings from a taxed jump in demand in the economy might look like. And whether and at what levels of basic income people exit the formal labour market. And whether that even matters with this altered vision. And whether, as I mentioned earlier, we first need to find alternative and equally powerful sources of dignity. Not everyone can play in a band.

Some related and overlapping exercises look at what assumptions we are taking for granted, what is common sense here and what would its rejection look like, what would you do if the immovable barriers you take for granted didn't exist, and similar approaches. This set of exercises approaches the same problem as the previous one but in an analytical, exploratory way.

Various exercises take the form of Dreamers vs. Realists (Good cop/Bad cop, Red team/Blue team), role plays in which one team makes up impossible improvements to the world and the other plays devil's advocate, forcing increments of adjustment from fantasy to reality. A third team can be judges and note takers. Work through the stages from proof of concept to prototype to pilot to go to market. Make up competitors if there aren't obvious ones to hand. Team three votes at each point on whether to progress to the next stage. Then make the teams swap roles.

A very commonly advocated exercise, which nobody believes will work until they try it, is random word mind mapping. Again, split into two or three teams. Each picks a random word from the dictionary. Then mind-map out ten instant associations. No delays. Turn one of the associations into a solution. Keep doing that until the time runs out. Pick the best one and pitch it. The point of any exercise with a random element like this is that it takes us to completely unexpected starting places.

Why haven't the effects of technology been captured here as they have been elsewhere?

This is one of a number of exercises that challenge an assumption that has the more general form of, 'We are different because. . . '.

I have rarely worked with a company, government agency or third-sector organisation that does not have a very understandable yet almost entirely misguided sense of its own uniqueness. This misapprehension is all the more difficult to see or challenge from inside the organisation because it is often the product of a strong, positive culture which serves the organisation well in other areas. Yes, you are unique in so many beautiful ways. But that doesn't mean that you can stop innovating with all the tools available to you, and particularly in a way that respects the rising expectations of your customers or citizens, driven by the kinds of service they are receiving elsewhere. External provocateurs, like consultants, can be useful here.

Every organisation of any size is also very likely to be constrained by the awful state of its data; its consistency, accuracy and accessibility. Back-office systems, particularly around enterprise resource planning (ERP) and customer relationship management (CRM), are generally out of date, poorly implemented and poorly understood. Not to mention, guarded, filtered and siloed in the service of conflicting managerial narratives.[11] Yet many of the next wave of innovations that promise to harvest the immense power of AI, machine learning and visual correlative analytics of various kinds is literally inaccessible without the prior data work being properly undertaken. There is no point in doing wonderful innovations in these areas without preparing the organisation to benefit from it – unless you are doing it for aesthetic or professional development reasons (as many are). Capacity for and timeliness of creation in this context allow or preclude subsequent adoption and implementation. It is also worth bearing in mind what some of the limitations of LLMs might be when we start to use their obscurely sourced products closer to the heart of the business. LLMs do correlation, not causation. There's no reasoning where there is no free will, which is why these systems are 'weak causal parrots'.[12]

What would magic look like here?

I have used this question as a placeholder for the various ideation and brainstorming exercises that attempt to discover the hidden barriers to our creative thinking by starting from an irrational place. Take one immovable obstacle to change and pretend for a while that you could use magic to remove it. What one wish would you use your genie to grant at work? You're allowed to change your boss if they aren't playing but you have to say why. We might describe this approach as the 'Mary Poppins' school of creative thinking.

In 2013, I had been talking to my friend Indy Johar about transparency and accountability on and off for months when I hit a minor crisis by having been summoned at short notice to give evidence to a UK Parliamentary Select Committee on corporate governance and regulation. These unexpected external forcing events are only valuable if the groundwork has been put in place. Indy is a high-energy, contemplative architect and serial social entrepreneur and one of the many founders of the impact hub movement in the early 2000s. He had already spent years exploring the meanings and applications of 'openness'. His mind was prepared. He could think structurally. He understood markets and platforms. He understood Openness deeply. And he understood the implications of the problem at hand.

In other words, I was asking the right question of the right person at the right time. I asked him 'What one simple idea can I give them that will create the conditions to make firms more transparent again, to go back to the bargain we struck when we created the limited liability company?' It helped a lot that we were both working in the Westminster Impact Hub at the time and were surrounded by young enterprises trying to solve a bunch of overlapping and related social problems around sustainable investment, wiki-building and urban design, time banking and alternative currencies and (literally) a thousand other things. It's hard to overstate the importance of clusters in creating the conditions for creative thought. Proximity breeds serendipity.

Indy thought for a while and then replied, 'Why not break the private sector in half so that we have a private sector and an open sector. The open sector would be completely transparent about everything including ownership, pay, supply chain, investments, political donations, etc. Membership would be entirely voluntary – companies could choose which sector they wanted to be in. But we would reward the more onerous reporting obligations of the open sector with lower taxes and perhaps an advantage in government tenders. And those rewards would be augmented by consumer appeal in certain areas.' That is a very simple, very powerful idea. We riffed a little on it and he published the idea on *Medium*.[13] You need people like this on your innovation team. People who can listen deeply to what the people around them are wrestling with and then generate ten amazing ideas, at least nine of which will be completely unworkable. We spent some effort on adoption and implementation, but we haven't got there yet. It remains a great daydream waiting in the ether to become an innovation. Meanwhile, Indy put a seriously diverse team of practitioners and designers around him and called it Dark Matter, a rapidly expanding public purpose innovation practice focussed on sustainability innovations around participative urban design and reimagining the boring stuff that holds us all back in financing, governance, resource allocation, ownership and beyond.

I want to stress that the beautiful link of creativity in the chain of innovation is worth nothing without the other links. There are many linear models or even linear models decorated with feedback loops that attempt to capture and simplify the process of moving through the chain of innovation, and broadly speaking they all take the form of moving from ideation to proof of concept to prototype to pilot to project to programme to movement.

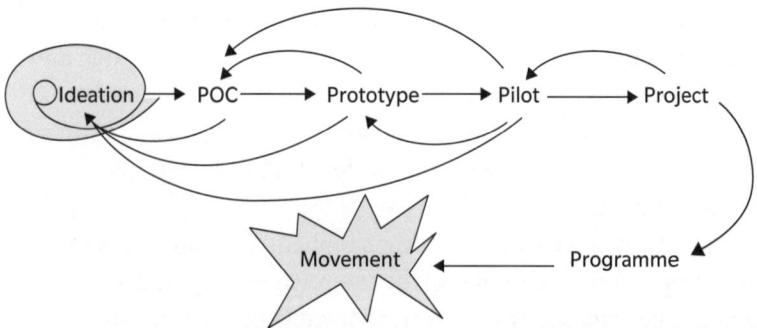

And this is a useful schematic to keep in mind as long as we understand that the deeper requirements to create, adopt and implement need to be informing and conditioning our actions at each of these stages. And just as the purpose of our work both drives and guides us through each of these stages, so does the obsession with endless iterative testing and, where possible, user testing and the dynamic ethnography of understanding customer responses to our unfolding innovation. The names we give the stages and the particular spiral path that this creative unfolding takes are less important than getting our mission, our approach and our people rightly aligned to change the future. And, as will become clear, these steps often lie in different organisations and sectors, and the extent to which the innovator can always orchestrate the entire chain will depend on a range of variables.

What if we have great ideas but not enough money?

There has never been a group of innovators who thought they were sufficiently well funded and didn't lament at length what wonders they could achieve in the world if only the idiots with the money would hand large amounts of it over to them as soon as possible. In fact, sadly it appears to be a critical success factor for innovation groups of all kinds to be egregiously underfunded in the early stages, as if they didn't have struggles enough already. Enforced frugality just short of complete bankruptcy turns out to be a catalyst for creativity without compare. And yet it's clear that the unparalleled availability of capital in Silicon Valley is one of its most marked comparative advantages. Where does the truth lie?

A particularly piquant example is provided by Skype. Struggling Swedish entrepreneur Nik Zenstrom had rebased himself in London, his co-founder Janus Friis was in Copenhagen and their three first engineers – Ahti Heinla, Priit Kasesalu and Jaan Tallinn – were all based in Estonia.

They had already used up virtually every last bit of credit they could get their hands on after unsuccessfully stopping the entertainment industry from suing KaZaH, their first-generation P2P music sharing company, back to the stone age. They were trying to collaborate between their three cities ultra-cheaply and couldn't find a stable, workable Voice over Internet programme. So, they made one up and called it Skype. And sold it to eBay 2 years later for $2.6 billion. When Zenstrom is asked by would-be entrepreneurs what main advice he would give he says, 'It's more important to have smart people who really believe in what you're doing than really experienced people who may not share your dream.' That's the purpose point again. But he also says, 'You need a cheap room with cheap chairs in it.' Nowhere does he recommend having a Foosball table.

Time and again we find frugality operating as a forcing function for innovation. But let's not get caught up in simplifying myths. Everybody loves the story of lavishly government-funded Secretary of the Smithsonian, Sir Samuel Pierpont Langley's 'Great Aerodrome', which 'flew like a handful of mortar' through a vertical flightpath into the Potomac river on 8 December 1903. The *New York Times* editorial, in ridiculing Langley's folly, surely achieved one of the all-time great journalistic predictions when it wrote that it would likely be 'a million years' before the technical problems could be overcome. Nine days later Orville and Wilber Wright made the first manned flight for 59 seconds in the Kill Devil Hills of North Carolina. How could we not love the story of a pair of bicycle repairmen from Ohio who hadn't finished high-school beating someone with a knighthood and $50,000 in government war research funding?

Without wanting to take away from Simon Sinek's superb use of the story to drive home the point about purpose,[14] it turns out the truth is a little more complex. Although he came late to the challenge, Langley had already done nearly two decades of publicly funded experimentation, building on earlier achievements in Australia, France and Germany. He had a series of breakthroughs in unmanned flight and also narrowed down some of the areas that needed solving as well as eliminating some of the possible solutions. And he'd got so close that after minor adjustments the 'Great

Aerodrome' was later successfully flown manned by Glenn Curtiss over Keuka Lake in 1914 as part of the subsequent patent dispute with the Wrights.[15]

What is more to the point is that the Wrights built on that work in a number of ways and were able to narrow the focus of their enquiry. In 1899 they wrote to the Smithsonian who sent them all their research papers on the subject. When Langley wrote to the Wrights asking if he could visit Kitty Hawk to learn from their experiments, they turned him down. Without taking anything from the brilliance of the Wright's amateur engineering and the passion of their mission, this is a story that has been repeated often. Mariana Mazzucato's tour de force, *The Entrepreneurial State*, provides many similar examples. Particularly memorable is the diagram showing where in the US Government virtually every element of the iPhone comes from with DARPA responsible for DRAM cache, micro hard drive, microprocessor, the internet and SIRI; various other military agencies for multi-touch screen, Navstar-GPS, cellular technology, LCD and signal compression, while the European publicly funded CERN developed HTTP and HTML, the foundation protocol and language for the World Wide Web.[16] Einstein may have been unusually modest but no less near the inescapable truth of every great figure in the history of innovation in claiming that he stood on the shoulders of giants.

The innovation group I worked in at Cisco applied a well-tested hybrid solution to this conundrum. We were lavishly funded for core innovation staff with a diverse set of experiences and skills, but anybody wanting to run an innovation beyond the proof-of-concept stage had to win funding from another part of the company, or another company or foundation or government. This meant that the core team was world class and felt reasonably secure as long as they were high performing, but that they had to struggle hard to win funding for any of their ideas to take off.

Mindlab in the Danish Government pursued a similar strategy for over 20 years, and we find similar models wherever we look, whether it's Lockheed's skunkworks, Xerox PARC or the team that Malcom McLean put together to drive containerisation, the best people he could find in the cheapest office he could find, deep in debt and fighting to keep his Citigroup lenders off his back. Even successful start-ups generally pay to get the best people they can get their hands on, and in the early days before that's possible they pay instead with disproportionate shares of future equity. It could be that one of the several structural reasons that governments struggle so much with innovation is that they do the exact opposite of this proven model by underpaying their people and over-funding their projects. And if you want to waste egregiously large sums of money, you could do worse than adopt the normal government approach to the chain of innovation diagram:

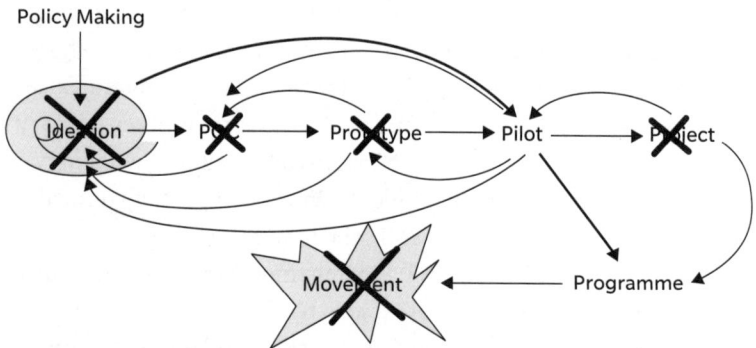

Notes

1 13 December 2015, www.ladbible.com

2 Come to Us, Creative Spirit | Hymnary.org

3 https://en.wikipedia.org/wiki/Post-it_Note

4 Bason, LPSI, pp. 171–189.

5 Gerd Gigerenzer, a prize-winning behavioural scientist at the Max Planck institute for human development, has argued that while the original insights about the limits of rational choice theory were valuable, much of the recent nudge work is not only paternalistic but potentially misleading and subject to 'bias bias' i.e. looking for and finding biases that aren't there. 'Unknown

to most economists, much of psychological research reveals a different portrayal, where people appear to have largely fine-tuned intuitions about chance, frequency and framing. A systematic review of the literature shows little evidence that the alleged biases are potentially costly in terms of less health, wealth, or happiness. Getting rid of the bias bias is a precondition for psychology to play a positive role in economics.'

Gigerenzer, Gerd, The bias bias in behavioral economics, *Review of Behavioural Economics*, December 2018. https://www.now-publishers.com/article/Details/RBE-0092

6   I went to University with Mr Johnson and these characteristics were already well established in his early 20s.

7   Sanders et al., LAFTR, 109433. Sanders et al., NTC, 2023.

8   Sodha, *The Guardian*, 26 April 2020.

9   Goffman, *OTR* 2014.

10   McKenzie, *GB*, Policy Press, 2015.

11   As my old friend Grant Johnson points out, salespeople almost never put a true picture into Salesforce (SFDC) and other customer relationship management (CRM) and sales management systems for fear of theft, reallocation and various forms of management 'involvement'. I never met a good salesperson (and I've had the pleasure of working with many exceptional ones) who didn't run a private Excel spreadsheet to keep track of reality, making SFDC literally a net destroyer of productivity as well as a constant source of management delusion. Which would explain why it's literally never aligned with the actual accounts tracking receivables.

12   Zečević et al., CP.

'Some argue scale is all what is needed to achieve AI, covering even causal models. We make it clear that large language models (LLMs) cannot be causal and give reason onto why sometimes we might feel otherwise. To this end, we define and exemplify a new subgroup of structural causal model (SCM) that we call meta SCM which encode causal facts about other SCM within their variables. We conjecture that in the cases where large language models (LLMs) succeed in doing causal inference, underlying was a respective meta SCM that exposed correlations between causal facts in natural language on whose data the LLM was ultimately trained. If our hypothesis holds true, then this would imply that LLMs are like parrots in that they simply recite the causal knowledge embedded in the data. Our empirical analysis provides favoring evidence that current LLMs are even weak "causal parrots."

13   darkmatter. provocations. opensector

14   Sinek, How Great Leaders Inspire Action, *TedX Puget Sound*, 26 June 2013.

15   Dr Russ Naughton and Professor John Bird, both of Monash University, have pulled together a superb complete referenced timeline at the Hargrave archive now hosted at the Australian National Archive. http://www.ctie.monash.edu.au/hargrave/langley.html

16   Mazzucato, TES, p. 109.

chapter 5

—

Build alliances or all your time is wasted

'By the time the deviation becomes "statistically significant" and thereby visible to the planner, it is too late. Innovative opportunities do not come with the tempest but with the rustling of the breeze.'

Peter Drucker[1]

There are a number of great strategies for introducing and protecting innovation inside non-innovative organisations.

You will always need very senior stakeholder protection – preferably right from the top or as close to it as you can get. Without it, you will be killed. There isn't really a way around this. People who try usually end up leaving and becoming entrepreneurs – which is a completely different thing. Most senior executives and all strategy consultancies preach this by the way. But practise it not so much.

The bandwidth of ministers, directors general, CEOs and EVPs is obviously extremely limited but probably even more than most of their staff realise. And the more pressing the organisational need for innovation becomes, the higher the flames are burning on the deck if you like, the more limited that bandwidth becomes. Occasionally leaders emerge who understand this and find strategies to deal with it, but even those who have known it before are likely to become engulfed in the day to day.

I remember discussing climate change and the complex sustainable urban development initiative we had developed with the deeply thoughtful Satish Narayanan, who worked in the Clinton Whitehouse, about how innovative strategies can come to the attention of, let alone receive the blessing of, senior leaders. He said 'All governments, I believe, begin with a robust planning process and try to integrate ongoing inputs into that . . . You don't understand what it's like. Virtually every day is consumed by the absolutely compelling need to address the things that are going wrong that very day or in the next day or two. Everything that has not been institutionally set in train is in the moment. Survival and the avoidance of humiliation or catastrophe is for today. Strategy and innovation is for the day after tomorrow. And the day after tomorrow never arrives. Of necessity only the most nimble and evolving strategies take shape.'

It might be illustrative to walk quickly through the key steps we took to get full CEO buy-in and executive air cover at Cisco for an innovation programme predicated on a fundamental analysis the CEO didn't even agree with; that climate change presented a real threat and a strategic business imperative, rather than a tree-hugging distraction to a company, which, on the face of it, made hardware-imbedded software to make the internet go faster.

Firstly, you have to prepare the minds of the advisors your prospective executive sponsor may turn to for advice. Unearth likely key objections or misunderstandings and get them answered or cleared up in advance. It's far harder (to the point of impossible) to undo the damage of a key advisor telling the executive your initiative is a bad idea because they are missing key information or, frankly, just because they're pissed off that it wasn't their idea or that they weren't consulted. Flattering them with respect in advance is a far more efficient use of your time. To achieve this, you will need a senior Advocate/Sherpa, someone who knows their way around the e-suite and, for whatever reason, is a passionate believer in your innovation. She should be highly politically astute and know what makes her colleagues tick.

Secondly look for external authorities with little or no agenda that your sponsor is likely to respect. We had an accidental breakthrough when we lured our CEO into a meeting at NASA Ames where he got to look at unmanned flying prototypes, hyperwall steerable supercomputing and wind tunnels as big as small towns and ended up in a conversation with Pete Worden, Ames Director, a truly great innovator and scientist, former US Airforce Brigadier General and Arizona University Astrophysics Professor (now appropriately chairman of the Breakthrough Initiative Prize Foundation set up by Yuri Milner and Stephen Hawking among others).

Pete had won great recognition inside NASA for his innovations in low-cost, light, fast, small satellite development in the late 80s and 90s, which partly depended on his ground-breaking advocacy of flat, diverse, respectful organisations focussed on rapid prototyping. One of his many achievements had been the Clementine lunar mapping mission, which established that there was sufficient crater water on the moon to support human habitation and spacecraft refuelling. Pete represented the very best of the kind of practical, innovative, deeply scientifically grounded government advisor that had made the US such a great centre of innovation and economic growth in the twentieth century before they more or less completely lost their way.

After the flying things and lunar modules and wind tunnels, my CEO sat down with Pete and, reaching for some kind of common ground, as is his genius, asked him why the Alaskan wild salmon he loved to fish had been swimming upriver later each year. Pete explained that climate change was impacting the Sockeye in five different ways. Warming waters off the Pacific Northwest coast confused navigation into the Bristol Bay system while ocean acidification through excess absorption of carbon dioxide was slowly degrading the Sockeye food chain. If they did make it up into the freshwater system, warmer river waters increased disease and predation. Meanwhile the melting retreat of upriver glaciers reduced freshwater levels, which made it harder to reach spawning grounds, while increased extreme weather conditions also created hazards and obstacles. You could see the realisation on my CEO's face. Everything was connected and we were messing with god's creation. I'd love to say I'd planned that, rather than just learning from it. I call it permission innovation.

Thirdly, prepare to be able to pitch in 1 minute, 3 minutes and 10 minutes what you can defend for 3 hours. This is far harder than it sounds. Mastery of the art of the pitch is a requirement not limited to those entrepreneurs doing seed or early round investments. It is fundamental to every innovator building stakeholders and sponsors in a large organisation or complex environment. The problem is that you need to have mastered your argument in sufficient depth to be ready to answer a thousand potential questions, and it is hard to reduce that amount of knowledge to the essence of the pitch. My urban innovation team (headed by the *inarrestabile* Nic Villa) came up with the industry's first smart city construct. They were asked to prepare the minimum key information to justify CEO buy-in and possible investment, they worked for weeks and boiled it down to an 87-slide PowerPoint deck. And believe me when I tell you that some of those slides had packed in a whole lot of information.

The iterative work of going from a strong new idea, down deep into its foundations, justifications, technical and market analyses and then back up to an accessible crystallisation rooted in that knowledge is one perhaps only learned over time. But everyone pushing to do something new against institutional barriers will meet it myriad times. Three things will guide you: the limited bandwidth of the executive, the focus on what they care about in language they feel comfortable with and the continuous return to your guiding purpose. This brings together in a moment of truth all the elements we have spoken about already: the purpose, the close-knit, diverse, mutually respectful high-performance team, the focus on customer or citizens' unmet needs, the financial, material and technical constraints and the endless iteration.

Having gone through all of the previous steps, the story we ended up telling, in its totality, on the basis of those 87 slides was as follows:

For hundreds, if not thousands of years, cities, which are now where most of us live, have been built around the idea of a central marketplace. The centralised replacements of the coffee house or trading square remained the urban organising principle, and all traffic and transport systems, business and housing systems, energy and power systems were influenced by this idea that people meet at the centre to trade pigs, flowers, ideas, skills, insurance contracts, etc. With the pervasive connectivity you helped to make possible, the city doesn't have to be that way anymore. We can have a distributed city, a multi-centre city, where work, ideas, skills, money and power move to where they are needed. This will be far less carbon intensive, and will unlock huge time efficiencies that people can give back to their friends and families, improving their quality of life. And finally, and crucially, it will be good business for us, increasing demand for distributed, packetised or virtualised energy, transport, work and living systems.

It's not quite as pithy as 'picture snakes on a plane' but it takes only one leisurely minute. Architecting permission to proceed is pitching to be allowed to pitch. For longer and to other people. All the way to permission to pilot.

It is well worth keeping your intentions well hidden from most people until you have achieved critical velocity. Many innovations are not best served by being analysed while they are still nascent, and the failure rate has to be much higher than the rest of the organisation can tolerate, or you aren't innovating. This respect for failure and its relationship with innovation is widely understood in principle but seemingly hard to tolerate in practice. Why is this? I think there are a couple of reasons.

The archetypal case study in this area is Lockheed Martin's Skunk Works. This was set up in Burbank, California in 1943 by legendary aviation engineer, Kelly Johnson, and was given its name as a joke derived from Lil Abner's moonshine 'Skonk Works' by early recruits because it was warehoused next to a foul-smelling plastic factory. The initial scramble was to design as fast as physically possible a jet fighter superior to the best of German air power.

Kelly negotiated the terms under which he would attempt this near impossible feat and he and his successor, Ben Rich, managed to keep them more or less in place for the next 50 years and more. The concept has been copied and replicated in over 50 companies since, but it appears that some of the key components of the agreement have rarely been fully achieved or even fully understood. Kelly summarised the deal in 14 basic operating rules which he wrote after a few beers with close colleagues in 1943. The key ones for our purposes here are:

1. The Skunk Works programme manager must be delegated practically complete control of his programme in all aspects. He should have the authority to make quick decisions regarding technical, financial or operational matters.

3. The number of people having any connection with the project must be restricted in an almost vicious manner. Use a small number of good people.

5. There must be a minimum number of reports required, but important work must be recorded thoroughly.

11. Funding a programme must be timely so that the contractor doesn't have to keep running to the bank to support government projects.

14. Because only a few people will be used in engineering and most other areas, ways must be provided to reward good performance by pay not based on the number of personnel supervised.

These were then locked in place with executive sponsorship based on the complete trust in Kelly by CEO Robert Gross, which derived among other things from an incident in 1932 when Kelly, aged 23, had called bullshit on the then chief engineer for inherent instability in their core twin engine design. This led directly to their trademark twin tail arrangement and the likely saving of the company. We can't all stumble upon that kind of opportunity to secure executive support, but it gives you an idea of the kind of courageous approach you could aspire to.

The link between CEO and the Skunk Works was also guaranteed by Kelly's unconventional dual role as chief engineer of the company between morning and mid-afternoon and Director of the Skunk Works from then into the night. This whole arrangement was strong enough to sustain them through their second and third projects, which were catastrophic failures. (One was a vertical take-off jet that could take off safely but tragically could not land again.) They went on to build the U2 and many other breakthrough successes as well as many failures.

All the diverse skills represented there were jammed deliberately close to each other in extremely frugal quarters so that designers and engineers would be close to the iterative prototype build. Dress was casual and hierarchy irrelevant just as pay was based on skill, not on how many people you managed. Total executive protection from the corporation and its politics and processes, elite recruitment, small tight teams, constant iteration, stable funding for good people but frugality for everything else and a very clear mission driven by a strong leader with fanatically devoted team members. Kelly was famous for firing people during disagreements. They would completely ignore this and come back to work next day, and he would never say a word. He was also famous for recruiting brilliant people who didn't fit in most places so constant firing was an unconventional but strangely appropriate management tool.

It's instructive to compare this story to the legendary Xerox PARC and see what patters we can draw out from both as well as our experiences at Cisco Systems. In the late 60s Xerox was riding high, awash with cash and aware, perhaps for the first time, of the possibility of a competitive threat from IBM. They invested a vast amount of money in the wrong tech company, Scientific Data Systems, and then tried to make good on the investment by setting up a blue-sky research facility in Palo Alto. Two things went their way. ARPANET, the government-funded precursor to the internet, was already up and running with a grand total of four nodes. And the government, mired in an increasingly hopeless and expensive Vietnam war, had started to tighten funding for original research after a long period of generous, patient, early-stage investment.

Those golden years had been partly presided over by the legendary JCR 'Lick' Licklider, an MIT behavioural psychologist who pursued his mission to improve man/machine interfaces at the Pentagon ARPA funded IPTO (Information Processing Techniques Office). He recruited Bob Taylor who had worked in the aerospace industry on designing Pershing missiles and flight simulators before spending several years at NASA on the moon-shot team. Roberts inherited Lick's obsession with improving machine usability and information management and he also inherited his huge research budget. He applied it up and down the country on funding basic research in computing, visualisation, data management and networking. When Xerox PARC recruited him, he knew and was loved by every brilliant person in the country doing basic research in the emerging fields that would contribute to the information revolution. Roberts brought to Palo Alto not only his prodigious Rolodex and his obsession with man/machine interface but an imperious sky's the limit, recruit the best, pay what you have to philosophy from the golden years at NASA and ARPA, and Xerox picked up the bill and offered CEO endorsement and protection for just long enough for them to invent the future of personal computing.

Within a year he had built a team the likes of which have rarely been seen before or since including Charles Thacker, co-inventor of ethernet, Bob Metcalfe, principal inventor of ethernet (and Metcalfe's law), Charles Simonyi, co-developer of WYSIWYG word processing, John Warnock who carried on PARC's mission by founding Adobe, Alan Kay, legendary pioneer of Object Oriented Programming and Graphical User Interface, Dan Ingalls, developer with Kay of the ground-breaking 'Smalltalk' programming language, Larry Tesler who later went to Apple and invented, among other things, 'copy and paste', Gary Starkweather, inventor of laser printing, Lynn Conway, co-developer of the silicon chip, Adele Goldberg, co-developer of Smalltalk, and many others.

Within 5 years they had invented or perfected nearly every aspect of modern accessible, democratised computing including desktop and portable computers, touch screens, graphics, windows, the mouse, laser printing, fast networking and the origins of modern modular object-oriented coding. Kay and Roberts shared an obsession with what was possible, which was part of the magic generated in PARC. 'Most of the inspired engineers Taylor recruited . . . the Lampsons and the Thackers, started out too blindly focussed on the issue of what was in their power to actually build. They would ask: what is the next stop on the road? Kay turned the question inside out: Let's figure out where we want to go and that will show us how to get there. He never lost sight of the computer's appropriate station in the world: *to conform to the user's desires, not the other way around.*'[2]

Taylor had few rules for his anarchic acolytes at PARC other than to work like crazy and be brilliant, but one activity was compulsory. This was the weekly 'Dealer' meeting, named after 'Beat the Dealer', where a single individual takes on all comers at Casino Blackjack. There team members had to present an idea or project proposal they were fond of to everyone else and withstand their collective attempts to tear it apart. The group worked without physical walls and without conceptual limits. If something didn't exist, they made it. If something was too expensive (like Bose speakers or a minicomputer) they made it. They were in several senses playing around while goading each other into literally inventing the future. Families were included in their frequent celebrations, barbeques, baseball games, touch football, poker and increasingly gaming, like 'Spacewar!', which featured centrally in a famous 1972 *Rolling Stone* article of the same name by Stewart Brand, founder of the Whole Earth Catalogue, who more or less invented the idea of the cool nerd.

And here we come to the problem, because as you have probably noticed, Xerox did not become the dominant company of the personal computer and internet age. When the *Rolling Stone* article hit the executives at HQ back east, it came after a series of arrogant missteps, budget over-runs and political mishandling, which meant the group and its executive backing were probably already doomed. And by then they were under competitive attack from Japan and no longer feeling so expansive about innovation, just at the exact time when it was most needed. But the most telling incident in Michael Hiltzik's fantastic account of this slice of history may well be the presentation I mentioned earlier, 'Futures Day' in 1977 when the PARC team got to present their work to the senior management of Xerox at the end of a company meeting. Long before any of these things existed, their live show included bitmapped screens, email for office workers, wireless laser printing, the mouse, collaboration software, windows, icons and graphical displays. Then they set up the first 30 personal computers in the world in a side room for the executives to play with.

Here is Charles Geschke, a programming genius who attended the demo: 'The typical posture and demeanour of the Xerox executives, and all of them were men, was this' – arms folded sternly across the chest. 'But their wives would immediately walk up to the machines and say, "Could I try that mouse thing?" That's because many of them had been secretaries – users of the equipment. These guys, maybe they punched a button a copier one time in their lives, but they had someone else do their typing and their filing. So we were trying to sell to people who had no concept of the work this equipment was actually accomplishing. It didn't register in my mind at that event but that was the loudest and clearest signal we ever got of how much of a problem we were going to have getting Xerox to understand what we had' (Hiltzick, p. 273).

The adoption and implementation stages of the chain of innovation were thus left to two young dudes who had heard about PARC's work. They were called Bill Gates and Steve Jobs. Jobs visited PARC twice at this time. Meanwhile, Xerox doubled down on being good at copiers. And speaking of copiers, here is how Bill Gates recalls it: 'The main "copying" that went on relative to Steve and me is that we both benefited from the work that Xerox Parc did . . . . We didn't violate any IP rights Xerox had but their work showed the way that led to the Mac and Windows.' (Gates on Reddit, AMA, 27 Feb 2017) One rough measure of the business cost of that mistake is that the combined market cap of those two little firms is now just shy of over $6 trillion. Last I looked, Xerox is at under $1bn and falling fast.[3] Just remember, if you work in a corporation of any size, you are 95 per cent likely to be working for today's version of those Xerox executives, and not for Bill and Steve. Buckle up.

I had a wonderfully smart, urbane colleague and co-conspirator at Cisco called Yvonne LeRoux. He was named in honour of his grandmother, who led the 'Reseau Johnny' resistance cell in the Port de Brest before being captured in 1942 and was subsequently one of 27 resistance heroes to be honoured on French postage stamps. Perhaps she is partly where he got his no bullshit approach to life and work from. He was in charge of the adoption stage of my group's innovations and navigated the corporate shark tank with grit, grace and diplomacy. With regard to innovation he frequently lamented the senior management's penchant for 'pulling up recently planted trees to see if the roots look healthy'. He was driven out of there eventually for his intelligence and honesty.

The challenge we face learning from these extraordinary lessons was beautifully summarised by Kelly Johnson's successor as head of Lockheed's Skunk Works, Ben Rich, commenting on the direction of corporate culture back in 1994. 'To buck smothering bureaucratic controls inside or outside government takes unusual pluck and courage. Smallness, modest budgets, and limiting objectives to modest numbers of prototypes are not very rewarding goals in an era of huge multinational conglomerates with billion-dollar cash flows. There are very few strong-willed individualists in the top echelons of big business – executives willing or able to decree the start of a new product line by sheer force of personal conviction, or willing to risk investment in unproven technologies. As salaries climb into the realm of eight-figure annual pay checks for CEOs, and company presidents earn stock options worth tens of millions, there is simply too much at stake for any executive turtle to stick his neck out of the shell. Very, very few in aerospace or any other industry are concerned about the future beyond the next quarterly stockholders' report.'[4] What would Ben say now?

You will need to find people outside your group who are going to get most, if not all, of the credit for your breakthroughs. The senior stakeholder becomes critical in this manoeuvre because somebody very senior needs to know who really created the breakthrough or you will be defunded in subsequent rounds. Let me repeat this point because it is really important. To survive in large organisations and complex environments, innovators absolutely must allow others to take the credit for their innovations. This is because the innovation group, almost by definition, will not have the resources and decision-making power to drive through the adoption stage to implementation and real-world iteration. Fully resourced innovation groups that can take each of the steps are rare and generally only occur in extreme circumstances where the government or company not only faces an existential threat but is fully aware that they do. Credit-giving is therefore frequently a fundamental adoption strategy.

If the senior leadership doesn't know where the innovation comes from, the catalytic group will lose its funding and the credit-taking group will win it. And a combination of ego, short-sightedness and stupidity, fuelled by perverse financial incentives, will usually ensure that they not only seek it, but sincerely believe they deserve it. The capacity of ambitious men to believe that the things that go well for them are down to their own unique brilliance knows absolutely no bounds.

A final word on adoption. The senior decision makers in most companies comprise white men in the last 5 or so years of their career. To get there, they have made many sacrifices and shown ruthlessness and determination. Faced with the risks involved in innovating new approaches or merely 'squeezing the lemon' they nearly always opt for the latter and behave completely rationally to maximise their large vested and soon to be vested stock holdings in a way that makes almost all interesting innovations anathema to them. In some ways this is good for the wider economy because in most situations not blighted by monopoly or near monopoly, it means their company will be destroyed in the not too distant future and replaced with better, hungrier, more innovative ones. Keep it in mind before committing slow professional deconstruction.

Notes

1   *IAE*, p. 255.

2   Hiltzick, pp. 82–83.

3   It's now $1.26bn. By the time this little book is published, you are going to be asking 'What Xerox?'.

4   *Rich & Janos*, p. 345.

chapter 6

Implementation – now for the hard graft

'I have been impressed with the urgency of doing. Knowing is not enough; we must apply. Being willing is not enough; we must do.'

Leonardo Da Vinci

Innovation without implementation is hot air. And yet it's very hard for some leaders to remember to value implementers just as highly as ideators, iterators, innovators, creators, 'design thinkers' and policy strategists. This is partly because these characters are much better at self-promotion and internal marketing than implementers are. But if you don't treasure your implementers, you will just make cool pilots and local one-offs that will make great marketing stories but achieve nothing real.

Even more important than valuing and nurturing implementors is baking your cake with a sustaining value model in mind. This might be profitability at some future point. It doesn't matter when that point is as long as you or your adoption curve can keep on persuading your corporate, public or venture investors that it exists. Or it might be social value through enhancing mutual respect, cohesion, social solidarity or justice. Or it may be some blend of the two where, for example, a negative externality is reduced or a positive externality sustained and enhanced.

Each of these adoption and survival models has one fundamental element in common. It doesn't matter whether you have reached or will soon reach profitability or are on your way to measurably improving the world. What matters is the perception (of where you will end up) by your sponsors or investors. Long before the endless losses of X (formerly known as Twitter), Malcom McLean pursued containerisation with passionate intensity and attention to detail and not once during his fights with his investors (First National City Bank of New York, now Citigroup) could he appeal to them for patience based on as yet unrecognised returns to investment. McLean's name is less well known than Zuckerberg, Gates et al., yet he and his team arguably did more to accelerate globalisation than anyone else. His multimodal standardisation innovation, creating containers compatible with trains, trucks, port stacking, cranes and boats, was introduced in New York in 1956. Estimates of the total ultimate effect on international shipping costs range from a 60 per cent reduction to a 90+ per cent reduction,[1] which is equivalent to a 5–10 per cent reduction in the cost of all transported goods everywhere. McLean was not the first to realise that standardised boxes could transform logistics, and several others had even tried it and concluded that it was impossible. By the time he started his play, McLean was running one of the largest and most profitable trucking companies in the US. There are many powerful lessons to learn from his travails, and I highly recommend Marc Levinson's wonderful book[2] on the subject. Here are a couple:

> **'Don't think about products and objects – think about systems and platforms. Solving the various design challenges in creating a true intermodal transportation system was not trivial but compared with solving the issues of being opposed by the government, the unions, the railways and other trucking and shipping lines, it actually was. One of the many ways McLean solved this was to make each essential standardised component that he could, patent free so that his competitors could adopt it without friction. He effectively gave the container design contract to the Freuhauf trailer company on the condition they provided them at the same price to all his competitors.'**

Don't think you can win sufficient investment with a business case. McLean's initial backer at Citi was a truly brilliant young trainee called Walter Wriston who would go on to become not just the preeminent banker of his generation and CEO of Citi but a true innovator himself in a number of areas of banking and a great one for speaking against regulation in public while shaping it hugely to his benefit in private. McLean and Wriston persuaded his banking bosses to lend $22 m so that he could solve the problem of not being allowed to be in both trucking and shipping by selling his trucking company and buying some ships.

Nearly every innovation of importance requires changes in the ecosystem. First, he negotiated peace with the longshoreman's unions of New York, no small feat in itself, ensuring both their safety and security and their subsequent support. Next in McLean's

79

battles was with the Port Authority of New York. They needed to fund the infrastructure that would make the handoffs between trucks and boats fast and profitable. Ultimately in the late 60s they agreed to put $322 million towards new port infrastructure in Elizabeth New Jersey. That's $3 billion in today's money. Government investment in the success of containerization didn't end there with McLean's new efficient shipping company winning the bulk of early contracts in the Vietnam war, both accelerating and entrenching his de facto global containerisation standards. As the Basques always say, 'judge the portfolio, not the individual projects.'

Don't try to predict or control the consequences of platform innovations. Interestingly the innovation consequences of containerization go even beyond their extraordinary impact on trade and globalisation. Two small ones; increasingly and ironically urban innovation spaces have been built out of containers, ideal for fast cheap, modular urban construction. At a more conceptual level, containerisation has revolutionised cloud computing by creating context neutral bundles of software which virtualize their own operating systems, making development more portable, agile, secure, fast and scalable.

Your stakeholders and funders will need to be comfortable with knowing that you are unlikely to have a better than one-in-seven success rate. Constant success and reports with 18 green traffic lights, 1 amber light and 1 red light are either just internal marketing or systematic, well-intentioned lying. In the public sector this need for comfort with failure is problematic to the point of impossibility, except where there is unusually enlightened risk-tolerant leadership or where all else has failed and utter destruction looms or where your senior manager is approaching retirement and actually doesn't give a good goddam.

It is hard but essential to build a culture where there is pride and reward for working well on one of the six failed initiatives and early project-kill decisions are not obstructed by passionate attachment. This takes strong leadership and, by extension, a huge amount of mutual trust in the team (see below). What is the key to making people feel proud of working on a 'failed' branch-line? Clearly the starting point is a pervasive sense of membership of a group with shared purpose. It is theoretically appealing to argue that each wrong turning eliminated early is a fundamental, per- haps even life-or-death, contribution to the potential success of the mission as a whole. But it's not going to feel that way to people who have poured heart and soul into a terminated endeavour. Goal scorers always get ten times the credit than goal savers get, despite their equal value.

Social start-ups

Given the nature of the challenges we face from climate change, unemployment, inequality and precarity and the related rise of populist politics as well as looming threats from social media abuse, AI and further automation, you might think that large foundations, principled high net worth individuals and families and governments might be jostling to fund social start-ups. Why aren't they?

The entire funding, measuring and incentivising structure of the social funding sector is more or less completely broken.

Innovation absolutely requires that teams be securely funded so that good people can be attracted and retained with stability through periods of experimentation. This core funding is virtually impossible to find.

Innovation absolutely requires an exploration and iteration that, by definition, cannot specify what the precise outcomes will be, when they will arrive and what their sustaining business model will be before the work is commenced. This unspecified outcome fund- ing is virtually impossible to find.

Innovation absolutely requires the possibility to fail often and early. Social funding that understands, tolerates or even welcomes this is virtually impossible to find.

Innovation teams absolutely require the best people you can find. Social funding absolutely requires you to pay as far below market rates as possible in a whole range of professional areas and relies on people either having family support or being prepared to live with extreme poverty and insecurity in return for the privilege of being poorly managed in pursuit of ill-defined goals within impossible resourcing constraints. This generally ensures that apart from a few extraordinary souls, the area will be largely staffed by the under-qualified, those attempting to achieve some kind of personal redemption or the lost and aimless offspring of the 1 per cent. As a recipe for failure this is pretty much fool-proof, which may be why real recent innovation in the social sector outside of government is virtually impossible to find.

There are many great exceptions to this such as the work of Filippo Addarii and his team in Milan and beyond, some of the projects supported by Nesta and the Young Foundation in the UK and Social Innovation Canada. We can perhaps particularly learn from Immy Kaur's incredible work with Civic Square in Birmingham with its focus on place making and equitable climate transition. There is no bigger or more extraordinary example than that provided by the Basque region over the last 40 years. I explore this case study at the end of this chapter. But for the most part social innovation has served mainly as a diversion of the energy of those who in previous generations would have had far greater impact by operating at the systemic political or commercial level.

Cluster luck

As one of my favourite thinkers once said, proximity breeds serendipity.[3] It's rare to come across a political leader who hasn't at one time or another come up with the startlingly original idea of creating a Silicon Somewhere. It's a relatively straightforward thing to do. You just have to find a place and put 'Silicon' before its name.

You will, of course, need to ensure that the weather is beautiful, land plentiful and cheap, a major financial centre is nearby and immigration enthusiastically encouraged. For a lot of that immigration, you will need a couple of generously funded world-class universities. It will take about 50 years for them to reach the kind of level you need. Make sure at least one of them is like Stanford, founded to accept men and women of any denomination with a distinctively practical and open philosophy at the heart of its success. At this point you're going to need two military crises of around the scale of WWII and the Cold War and then pour billions and billions of dollars of public funding into basic research into a whole range of areas like radar, aeronautics and basic electronics. It is only after you do that that venture capital is going to come in to reap the rewards of the first 100 years of your experiment. The entire VC industry in Silicon Valley in 1975 was $10m. Concurrently you will want your star university to break with all previous academic convention by encouraging and mentoring its brightest students to start companies and take any IP they want with them, more or less for free, on the understanding that it will serve the mission of defending the nation. That's where you'll get your first few Hewlett Packards. Now you'll have to slash your capital gains tax so that pension funds get drawn into the game. At the same time you'll need a Nobel-prize-winning inventor like William Shockley who invented the transistor, not only to move near to his mother, a female graduate of Stanford, but also to draw all the relevant leading scientists in the country to work for him and then manage them so shockingly that 65 'Fairchildren' companies are subsequently started by people desperate to escape either his company or Fairchild Semiconductor, started by the first eight to leave him.

So, to summarise, it takes about a 100 years, as much money as the government and particularly its military can spare, two national existential crises (or three if you separate the moon-shot from the Cold War), a beautiful climate and nice mountains and bays, a more or less completely open immigration policy (over 50 per cent of Silicon Valley start-ups were founded by immigrants) and a culture of openness, wild experimentation, play and general Californian idiocy. Good luck with that project.

In the UK they have tried this experiment at least four times but they keep ignoring the rules. 'Silicon Roundabout' in and around Old Street, Shoreditch and Hoxton started getting funding about the time there was no more cheap property. They did have a large local financial centre but its interest in tech start-ups, other than Fintech, was minimal. Cool shared working spaces and an abundance of artisanal coffee couldn't mask the lack of investment, the lack of critical information infrastructure and the lack of close ties to world-class STEM-focussed higher education institutions. There was no waterfall of public funding for basic research because the UK decided to ignore the real history of US innovation over the last 100 years, and wilfully believe instead the self-serving ideological dreams of its successful entrepreneurs, a costly error with endless consequences.

The good folk of Croydon, a city within the southern edge of London, had the cheek to start their own cluster. It had huge advantages over the Hoxtonites in that office property was plentiful and cheap and the group of founders and the entrepreneurs who joined them were genuinely diverse and driven. Their efforts were widely celebrated by politicians of every stripe and in the media. People were excited to see young folk who were not all white and middle class making this valiant effort. But they never received any funding at all from anyone.

'The Government literally spent more on talking about how good the cluster was than they did on the cluster. Despite their best efforts, and despite all of the support from government and the Mayor of London, they were unable to gather the support to sustain the Croydon Tech Hub, TMRW and were left to rely on the goodwill of volunteers. Without the local infrastructure, and without a skilled, local workforce, after five years of struggle the founders had to walk away exhausted.'[4]

Alternatively, you could look to cities and regions that have innovation strategies consistent with and deeply embedded in the narratives of their own culture, history and potential competitive advantages. There are many to learn from including Austen, Curitiba, Estonia, Melbourne, Milan, Scotland, Seoul, Shenzhen, Singapore and Toronto, to name a few at random, but it's not too

controversial to say that the Basque region in Spain is unique for
pursuing an innovation-based strategy that delivered over several
decades not just a huge number of successful and innovative start-
ups but a complete transformation in wealth, cohesion, equality
and quality of life. Between 1980 and 2010, largely under the governance of several cross-party alliances of sorts, Basque went from
being one of the poorest regions in Europe with over 40 per cent
unemployment, a collapsed heavy industrial economy and an active
separatist terrorist group to the second richest region in Europe, by
far the most egalitarian, with world-class clusters in advanced manufacturing, food production and packaging, tourism, sustainable
construction and mobility. For a deeper dive into this extraordinary
story, I highly recommend the forthcoming book[5] from my good
friend Gorka Espiau, visionary leader of the Basque innovation centre, Agirre Lehendakaria Centre for Social and Political Studies at
the University of the Basque Country – UPV/EHU in Bilbao. But it's
worth dwelling on some of the lessons Gorka and his former Eusko
Juarlaritza Lehendakaria, (Basque President) Juan Jose Ibarretxe
Markuatu have extracted[6] because they apply with varying degrees
to nearly every innovation challenge I have seen.

1 Progressive patriotism. Start with a pride in where you have come
   from that is liberating rather than restricting, a deep respect for
   your traditions as a source of inspiration and community convening, not a straitjacket. This allows for participative or inclusive
   innovation because it helps to bring people and their diverse skills
   with you. The Basques had a tradition of heavy manufacturing,
   which they turned through careful state investment into one
   of the most profitable advanced manufacturing and materials
   clusters in the world. The narrative bridges between the two are
   almost the only real thing that links them – advanced manufacturing requires completely different skills, materials, supply
   chains and higher education and training than building steel
   ships. It's one hell of a pivot. Understanding and respecting tradition in a company or town, region or country is a very different
   thing from inventing new traditions and fetishising them into
   ever more calcified rules. The extraordinary culinary innovations

of the modern Basques are strikingly different from the culinary gastrofacism you see with recent neo-Nazis like Matteo Salvini in Italy and his brethren in France and beyond. Innovation only thrives where there is freedom of expression and thought.

2 Tell stories. Strategies and policies are ok, but stories are equally or more important for inclusive innovation because as every successful leader knows, Martin Luther King failed with his first attempt to build a movement for transformation, best summarised in his now forgotten speech, 'I have a Strategy'.[7] Basque communities told stories rooted in a real and shared past that reached into an imagined and visionary future. After emerging from 40 years of brutal fascist dictatorship which had suppressed both the language and other expressions of national identity, these were stories of pride and identity, of a love of art and poetry and culture, of entrepreneurial spirit, creative, resilient, fiercely determined in the face of obstacles, solidaristic and inclusive, passionate about justice and fairness, the natural environment and food. There are many examples of this, but my favourite is the story of cooking. Basque men have a tradition of gathering to 'cook' in exclusive local clubs called Txokos or Sociedades. I put cook in inverted commas because although there was undoubtedly cooking taking place, by all accounts it was nothing too special on the culinary front. The clubs were more about creating men-only spaces to drink Txakoli and gossip, the way men of many cultures have done. Luna Glucksberg from LSE Inequalities provides a great definition. 'Groups formed by various quadrillas or groups of friends that purchase or rent a location and create there a specific space to have lunches, dinners and celebrations. These events usually take place in an atmosphere of gastronomic camaraderie that includes having lively informal group discussions, songs, card games and so on.'[8] Looping this key constituency into the transformation strategy was critical so the government decided to tell a story about how the Basques had always been brilliant cooks and they would fund a small number of young people to study in Michelin starred restaurants in France and be supported to set up their own restaurants on return. By itself this plan might have been an expensive

failure but combined with other strands of the renewal strategy, it became surely one of the highest return government investments of the modern era. Basque now has more Michelin stars per head of population than anywhere else in the world and people fly from all over the world just to eat there (and look at a little art).

3 Autonomy and freedom. Unlike the other, in 1980 when the Spanish national government was negotiating various levels of autonomy with the four 'historic communities' asking for it, Basque decided to take responsibility for their own taxation and consequent social expenditures. This was unquestionably a huge gamble at the time, given the 40+ per cent unemployment and an economy all but broken by deindustrialisation, globalism, terrorism and lack of investment. They had less to tax and more demands on their expenditure than almost anywhere in Europe at the time, and certainly more than Catalonia, Galicia and Andalusia. But they had economic autonomy and with it they pursued a stunningly successful industrial strategy.

4 Inclusion. Ronald Reagan in his last speech as president[9] offered a famous paean of praise to immigration that his fatuous descendants appear to have forgotten. You can go to France, Germany or Japan but you can't be French, German or Japanese, but if you move to America, you are American. Well in subtly different ways, the same is true of the Basque country. Basque nationalism has explicitly incorporated the inclusion of immigrants to the geographical area into its core concepts of citizenship,[10] partially a recognition perhaps of the commonality between the 'outsider' status of Basques historically and that of the immigrant, partly a recognition that their society, despite its strong sense of identity, has historically been enriched by waves of immigration and partly a typical belief of all innovators and revolutionaries, that these concepts are constructed and that we therefore have a choice in how to define them. This assumption in favour of inclusion permeates the innovation creation strategy at every level from the cross party advisory group surrounding President Ibarretxe from 1999 to 2009, to the policy on employing people with disabilities, which through the simple tool of excluding you from

all direct and indirect government contracts if you don't hit your employment quota as well as extra funding for companies that employ more than 70 per cent differently abled employees, has made Basque the only place in the world that I know of that has virtually full employment for this group (with large consequent savings in disbursements).

5 Innovation movements are almost always cross-sectoral. The architecture of Basque's industrial innovation strategy is complex, but some broad outlines are critical. I simplify it here as the simultaneous attention to three layers of infrastructure needed: institutional, physical and social. There are at least five government agencies associated with fostering innovation covering areas such as training, government investment, inward investment from EU and beyond, research and promotion and marketing. This might be called the institutional infrastructure of an innovation-centred industrial strategy. It is all the more remarkable that when you consider that this widespread industrial strategy was being pursued in the 1980s and 1990s, most of the rest of the world had become persuaded of one of the central tenets of neo-liberalism, that 'the best industrial policy is the one that doesn't exist', a comment on the Basque approach by Spanish Socialist Minister for Industry at the time, Carlos Solchaga. At the same time the government undertook a long-term programme of physical infrastructure relevant to both this part of the industrialisation and modernisation strategy and others. This included complete reimagination, reclamation and reconstruction of the docklands area devastated by unmanaged deindustrialisation, as well as transport systems, public and residential buildings and broadband, etc. On the next layer came the rebuilding and strengthening of social infrastructures, critically education and healthcare and social services essential to mitigating the risks of radical experimentation and entrepreneurialism. But probably most significant of these was one of the most comprehensive basic income schemes seen anywhere in the world and decades ahead of even basic safety net payments provision by the rest of Spain, introduced in 1989. A series of

social innovations that in turn created and nurtured an environment in which both services and product innovations flourished.
Perhaps the most famous and extraordinary example of collaborative industrialisation that explicitly rejects the hierarchical
and fracturing anomie of late capitalism is demonstrated by the
Mondragon cooperative cluster, a true physical instantiation of
the idea that anyone can innovate. Made up of over 200 interconnected cooperatives employing around 80,000 members/inves-
tors and including its own university, it was founded by a priest,
José María Arizmendiarrieta, from a small village with contributions from some of his parishioners in 1943. It now constitutes
a vast network of employee-owned and managed coops that
operates in 40 countries and includes heavy industry, advanced
manufacturing, software development, consulting, banking,
insurance and education among other things.[11]

6 Culture eats strategy for breakfast. Just as Drucker never said
 that,[12] I guess it's appropriate to end our brief tour of the extraordinary Basque transformation by debunking the 'Guggenheim
 effect'. The wildly popular theory of urban regeneration can be
 summarised as follows: Never mind what the public want. Make
 a bold elite decision to invest many, many millions in a unique
 flagship cultural palace that looks strange, ideally designed by
 a rockstar architect and soon enough your very poor post-indus-
 trial town will become the envy of the world and a destination
 for all. That's obviously all rubbish. Gehry's Guggenheim, started
 in the early 90s, was a brilliant piece of a much larger movement
 of culturally driven economic change, which included a lot of
 other architecture, painting, sculpture, poetry, music and food
 as well as interconnected actions across five levels; small and
 large communities, public–private collaborations, infrastructure
 and regulation impacting economic activity, the environment,
 education and social movements.[13] All connected to and giving
 three-dimensional form to the Basque's driving meta-narratives
 of creativity, resilience and transformation. Like those narratives,
 the Guggenheim itself is rooted in the past with its references to
 the steel and the ships built of it in that very location in the past

as well as huge and largely realised hopes for the future. Asked whether the famous 'Bilbao Effect' could be replicated, Frank Gehry said 'It cannot be applied. It would be necessary to replicate the culture, the people, the honesty, the clarity, the simplicity . . . in that project everybody was on board to make a better city . . . . If you want a Bilbao effect, study the culture, study the people.'[14]

And learn their pattern language.

Leadership and culture

'We know that this club is the mix of atmosphere, emotion, desire and football quality. You cut off one and it doesn't work.' 'I said I think it's impossible but because it's you boys there is a chance.' 'They are fucking mentality monsters.'

Jurgen Klopp, 7 May 2019, Anfield press conference

To some greater or lesser degree, every team will come to have a responsibility to be innovative. But the idea of a special team leading the innovation responsibility for an organisation will nearly always be useful as a catalyst to change both culture and outcomes. Judging the point when it becomes counterproductive to have a dedicated team is both critical and difficult. One of the ways organisations try to kill innovation teams is to allow innovation to be 'owned' as an excuse to continue with the relaxing pleasures of business as usual – i.e., to not collaborate with that team.

But another way to fight off the threat is to claim that the special group's work is so important that it is now to be diffused throughout the organisation. This is almost always untrue even if original intentions were good. Driving an innovation mindset through a large organisation is all but impossible and, in many cases, would anyway be counterproductive. Managers quite rightly want most of their teams to focus on doing really boring things repeatedly, as cheaply as possible. Most work is either tedious or pointless with the scale between the two tending to correlate to pay. To be clear for the benefit of those still at school, tedious work is low paid and pointless work is high paid, with various combinations in between. Rational decision makers therefore tend to try to move from low paid work to more highly paid work with graduates getting to start halfway. Most of these people don't have the incentives to innovate anything, although experience with low-paid tedious work is at least valuable raw material.

The best way out of this dilemma is for the group with catalytic responsibilities to carefully and deliberately build an explicit virtual team approach from early on, tapping the critically important diversity and front-line delivery skills and deep operational experiences of groups across and up and down the wider organisation, community or ecosystem. A virtual team is a team where people doing most of the heavy lifting are doing it unpaid and secretly, outside the parameters of their actual responsibilities. This addresses three problems: (a) the catalytic team is never given enough budget early on to recruit the skilled people needed because they can't prove that this level of expenditure has any return until they actually start doing the work; (b) it gets critical frontline and back-office experience fed into the innovation work, without which it will almost certainly fail; and (c) it makes the lives of the poorly paid less tedious and allows them to address some of the frustrations caused by lamentable management, disastrous processes, and arrogant and haphazard customer service.

Most organisations tend towards the recruitment of well-rounded, balanced individuals. As the builder of an innovation team, you will want some very imbalanced people who are weirdly outstanding in some way or other. Some of these may even be unbalanced people. You won't be able to innovate with a group of rule-following all-rounders. This is why you won't see any innovation at all coming out of any of the big consultancy firms, to pick one example at random. But to be fair, most organisations are incredibly bad at employing people who aren't mediocrities because they leave the selection up to senior management who recruit in their own image. The public sector used to be better at this because they would let almost anyone in and tend to promote more on merit than companies do so they end up with some really strange people in senior positions. Unfortunately, they have largely lost the benefits of this approach through 'professionalisation'.

A properly diverse team suffers from periods of mutual incomprehension bordering on all-out warfare because they will come from different backgrounds and inevitably not just speak different professional and cultural languages but value different things, value the same things differently and use different ways of valuing, regardless. Your job as an innovation leader is to stop this warfare and get them to see things from each other's point of view, which is incredibly hard to do. This gets even more exciting with international teams. It's not only that your engineers regard your designers as self-important flakes with nothing real to offer while your sales and business development professionals will look upon your strategy and ideation experts as an overpaid waste of corporate space Just as your delivery and customer service ninjas will look with blank incomprehension at your expert policy bores. But it is also likely that your Italians and French will regard your Germans and Dutch as lacking all imagination and creativity, your Scandinavians and Australians will deride the complete lack of clarity and directness of your Indians and Chinese. And just about everyone will despise the boundless arrogance of your English and Americans who even with second-rate degrees from third-rate universities seem to be convinced that they have been put on earth to tell the rest of the world how to do things.

You will need an almost insane conception of what is possible and therefore your team will need to radically expand their own belief in what they are capable of. To be able to do this, you will have to abandon almost everything people tell you about how to be a good leader, almost everything you have ever seen your own managers do and absolutely everything that supports the pervasively practised 'arsehole school of management' approach and follow these new rules below:

You can do everything right under the sun and have a budget that NASA's moon-shot team would have envied, but if you don't get the culture of the innovation team right, you will fail every time. There has been enough written on this subject to get to the moon without rockets, just by stacking management books end to end in a stairway to heaven. And nearly all of them are useless. Which is strange because it's actually not rocket science. There are just three things you need: good empowering leadership; amazing and diverse team members; and a powerful purpose-supporting culture. Get these three things right and you can actually shoot for the moon.

Our systems for choosing leaders in most polities and organisations are not just broken – they tend towards the success and promotion of people who are uniquely ill-equipped to be leaders by rewarding and promoting behaviours that are destructive of a generative culture and working environment. Most of us know this at gut level but accept it as an inescapable fact of life. A source perhaps of good conversational material with our friends in the bar or with our poor beleaguered families of an evening or weekend but not something you can do anything about. And it seems to be getting worse in many cases, presumably because we look up to who succeeds and assume that what we see betokens what we have to do to be successful ourselves. Worse than that, the power that accrues to our damaged leaders corrupts our culture in three ways. Firstly, it gives them amplified voice, both through status and the resources they command. Secondly it gives them the power to reward and incentivise, often unconsciously, the behaviours they so much admire in themselves. And finally, by undermining the clarity of our judgement as we 'agree' with them for career reasons as well as more human ones, as we tend to admire the strong and successful.

Let me give a contentious example from my own experience. I had the good fortune to work for several people when I was in Government that subsequently rose to the top of the British establishment and had the knighthoods to prove it. We got on very well and became and remained friends and my closeness to them undoubtedly benefited my career in many ways, providing me access, when I needed it, to the Prime Minister among others. They were utterly diligent men, ferociously bright, hardworking and model public servants to ministerial masters of varying political hues. But they were truly lamentable leaders, contributing in no small measure to a homogenous senior culture that barely managed to cherish even the appearance of diversity. And certainly, no diversity in thought; those that didn't naturally have the assured amateurish grace of the Oxbridge arts-educated middle-class male had to fake it (or imitate it) to succeed, which fortunately I could to some degree. They paid vague lip service to but had no understanding of or indeed interest in the challenges of leadership, very little knowledge of management and zero about the management of innovation. Technology and operations in general left them completely cold.

The effects of this were predictably catastrophic for the United Kingdom. The senior bureaucracy's systematic and wilful incomprehension of the nature of over-the-counter (OTC) markets, derivatives and many other relevant issues led directly to their underestimation of the seriousness of the financial instability that predicated the 2008 crash.

The subsequent advice or lack of it that led to the Brexit referendum and the consequent inexplicable lack of preparation for outcomes that parted company with wishful thinking was capped off with a catastrophic ignorance of the nature of geopolitical warfare in the social media age with consequences for the UK economy that may last for more than a generation. These are just two striking examples among many of the weakness of the cadre they helped to build. We will need to wait a while to find out how they contributed to thousands of unnecessary deaths during Covid. Super smart, super nice men who contributed as much as any did to the destruction of the UK's democracy and economy.

But you will rarely, if ever, hear or read a word of well-informed criticism of them or their colleagues. Why when it is so vital to our collective well-being? For the same reason you won't hear it of senior leaders in any sector until, drunk on their own imagined invincibility, they stray too far from acceptable norms. And even then, perhaps generally not. Because those who know enough to call out the behaviour have far too much to lose from doing so. And in remaining silent become complicit. And in becoming complicit they begin to build their internal justifications and defences and end up believing them or simply not thinking about it anymore. As we know, advanced techno-psychological research has established that our capacity to believe something that it is in our material interests to believe is almost infinite. How else could you explain why otherwise hugely intelligent people can argue with a completely straight face that unfettered financial reward is essential for incentivising the very rich, while the few crumbs needed to maintain basic dignity in life is deeply corrupting for the poor? The media are deliberately excluded from understanding this in both public and private sectors and may well lack the skills and experience to analyse it, even if they were allowed to see.

Let's start by looking at how we select and value leaders.

We value and celebrate those who go the extra mile. These people, by definition, live very unbalanced lives, undervaluing friends, family and community in the pursuit of ambition. They can be relied upon to put a deadline before a promise to a good friend or a partner. They can be relied upon to delegate time with their children to a paid surrogate or unpaid partner. Their focussed striving is deadening of their souls and destructive of the rich personal hinterland in which empathy and human understanding are rooted and can flourish. They are an irresistible gift to their organisation in the short term, but in the long term they lay the groundwork for a profound weakening of the organisation's culture in general and its capacity to innovate in particular.

We value and celebrate the ability to be in the right place at the right time. It's hard not to attribute superior powers to those who are fortunate, but these leaders go further than luck takes them. They are adept at taking credit for things they are not actually responsible for. The timing that decides when a good idea will work is way outside the powers of most individuals to influence. I watched in blank amazement in the three corporations I worked in as leaders were systematically rewarded for upturns in the market, combined with the extraordinary work of the engineers who made the products they sold. Then we exacerbate these already dolorous effects by promoting people for having the good sense to be tall or good looking or educated to speak with the reassuringly mellifluous confidence that is generally only gifted to those whose daddies could pay for it: luck compounded by luck amplified by dishonesty, greed and bad management.

We value and celebrate agility. You will observe in many successful leaders a career velocity that both masks and contributes to a deeper problem. Like successful consultants, they have become expert at not being present when the consequences of their actions and inactions become apparent. And thus, they have become experts in avoiding responsibility for the mishaps they have not prevented. I have returned again and again here to the integrated nature of innovation through chains from creation through adoption to implementation. A high-velocity leader, by definition, never carries through this complex chain of activities. Worse, they are often likely to seek to make a quick impact by tearing up or ignoring the efforts of their predecessors. And so, we are subject to endless cosmetic restructurings and vaguely missioned 'initiatives' that for the veteran worker will often appear remarkably reminiscent of earlier such efforts, the often-pointless product of previous cycles of self-serving, hyper-masculine leadership brand building, while rewarding with promotion the very people who failed us in the process.

We value and celebrate firefighting and the diving catch. Who has not witnessed the exhausting spectacle of a leader successfully taking credit for fixing a problem that they created or should have foreseen and forestalled in the first place? The unexciting business of slowly building cultural change is easily overshadowed by the fireworks of averting catastrophe. It is as if we are so relieved that the crisis has been successfully managed that we no longer have the will or the energy to ask why it occurred in the first place. And celebration is so much easier and enjoyable than holding people fairly to account. Some leaders even manage to build their reputations around being in the right place at the right time to execute the diving catch. There are conflicting theories about why an organisation like NASA, for example, was able to execute so flawlessly for so long. In the first two decades of its existence from a virtually standing start in 1958, NASA completed 31 consecutive expeditions into space without losing a single astronaut. It is surely partly because they had not just a culture of absolute excellence, but an unusually objective way of telling whether it was being demonstrated and an obsessive belief in testing that was deliberately put in place to filter out contractor bullshit. This is not a cheap approach, but it works.

We value and celebrate confident communicators. There is of course much to be gained from looking to our leaders to be able to communicate vision and strategy with clarity and confidence. But that's not the communication I'm talking about. The problematic leader is the one who is able to project confidence upwards, taking personal credit for their team's work and transferring blame for cock-ups to others. Low-bandwidth senior executives and sporadically convened boards are extremely vulnerable to these operators, lacking the time, energy or ability to look behind the marketing of the high-velocity leader to the nuanced complexity that lies below. Humility, subtlety and honesty are given less weight and less reward, and the ambitious are quick to learn how to best operate to their own advantage.

We value and celebrate knowledge and experience. It's a truism to say that many senior managers got where they are by excelling at a task several layers below the level they have been promoted into by mastering the skills listed here. This is particularly problematic in the digital area. The insecurity that often goes hand in hand with the kind of distorted personality required to get to the top in these systems means that our leaders are often very insecure about technical and other issues that are beyond them or developed out of recognition since they did have a grasp. It is particularly painful to watch a leader claim to understand the technical or professional details that those who work for him have mastered, thus giving him licence to occasionally interfere in coding or engineering or detailed policy making or whatever with lachrymose results that others have to quietly correct for. But perhaps it is even worse to see such leaders implicitly decide that what they cannot understand must be strategically unimportant.

We value and celebrate professionalism. In the absence of the energy or courage to engage in real strategic thinking or real creativity, we often turn in fear to the talismanic power of professionals and their pixie-dust processes. I am not of course talking about the essential professions that contribute so much to innovation, engineering, coding, design, architecture and the like. But rather the mystical leadership professions epitomised by business school graduates, economists, consultants and some of the emerging professionalised abuses of data analytics, the algorithmic arts and big data. Any leader that falls back on a 2 by 2 analysis or a spreadsheet and attendant graphs at the point where actual leadership is required has too often been rewarded for their analytical hard headedness.

We are prone to value decisiveness when we need consultation and consultation when we need decisiveness. This seems strange, complex and counterintuitive, but it's often observed. We too often see successful leaders who consult on what they have already decided on as a decorative function or afterthought, a prophylactic against potential criticism. This is upside down and corrodes trust as well as generating weak decision making.

We promote and value leaders who say 'You cannot manage what you can't measure.' Data and metrics are much like processes – very useful in the service of good judgement. But an organisation that only manages what it is able to measure is on the fast train to Stupidville. Extraordinarily the quote 'If you can't measure it, you can't manage it' comes from the truly great management thinker W Edwards Deming in *The New Economics* and what he actually said was 'It is wrong to suppose that if you can't measure it, you can't manage it, a costly myth.' The Deming Institute continues to struggle to defeat this profound misunderstanding[15] with little apparent success.

Deming long before others realised that performance appraisals were deeply damaging. The interesting thing is that he was a statistician by training and thus understood the power *and limits* of metrics. Strong tools in the hands of the amateur are a danger to all. Most business intelligence (BI) tools and emerging AI are particularly dangerous in the hands of amateurs. Most users in the public sector are amateurs or close because the public sector can't afford professionals in this area at present. Consider some of the things you can with benefit measure: sales, cost of sales, total cost of sales, addressable market, market penetration, days of absence due to sickness, returns due to faults, average time on a call to a call centre, six sigma compliance, monthly active users, return customers, etc. All very valuable at certain points and times of doing business, all completely irrelevant to the early and middle stages of innovation. Now imagine trying to create practical metrics for the following: attentiveness, open mindedness, scepticism, customer/citizen focus, customer/citizen love, passion, collaboration, inquisitiveness, playfulness, beauty, elegance, natural fit, grit and resilience, generosity, etc. Don't try too hard, but never make the mistake of undervaluing all these and a bunch of other qualities as central to high-functioning innovation teams just because they can't be measured. If you can't measure it, you may be able to lead it.

We promote and value leaders who use the term 'human resources'. This is beginning to change slowly now but it is a remarkable testament to the nature of our approach to work and leadership that we allowed for so long the use of the term 'human resources' and everything associated with it. What the hell is a human resource? Somebody who is not using AI? There are a lot of ways you might imagine a group that managed recruitment, training and employee flourishing in a way that was good for all. Sometimes it feels like 'HR' departments are full of people transferred there because they lack all relevant and useful skills for the rest of the business and then develop, semi-drunk on the power they exert over people's day-to-day survival, a lax mendacity that is absolutely toxic for the entire culture of the organisation. It's probably much more complicated than that. I suspect that HR departments, like Finance and IT, often are the last to garner real investment and the first to suffer real cuts. The professionals who go there with a passion to transform the organisations they work in end up fighting endless fires caused by badly implemented ERP, payroll and workforce management systems, and navigating around the endless complex screw-ups caused by arrogant and often untouchable senior managers. There's a whole separate book to write about the billions if not trillions of dollars of lost productivity caused by ignorant short-term investment decisions made about 'back office' functions in most companies, nearly all government departments and agencies and every single charity on the earth. But at least they are valued by executives, like compliance departments in financial services companies, for being a group that is always at hand to take the blame when things go wrong and never in need of any real credit when they don't.[16] I must get this manuscript cleared by my HR department before it goes to publication so you very likely won't get to read this paragraph. Or if you do have that pleasure, you can assume I am now 'running my own boutique consultancy. . .'.

We admire and reward 'great networkers'. Some people are fabulous joyous connectors with a natural curiosity about others, generous with their own insights and connections. But I think you know the leaders I'm talking about, those who know how to work the room and have a business card collection the size of the Library of Congress to prove it. They have weaponised upward networking and it's not a pretty sight. I had the misfortune to be dragged along to Davos one year as the fake partner of my CEO partners travel free and we were a struggling start-up). There were a lot of other fake CEO partners there, but they looked strangely different from me (and they weren't there to network). I felt initial euphoria of arriving into the final inner compound, populated only by the 2500 richest, most powerful people in the world plus a few momentarily tolerated artists and vogue thinkers and some third-sector guilt icing. As the lowest of the high, I quickly became aware of the nature of the event. Each person there was continuously, desperately and cravenly attempting to achieve a little facetime with someone more powerful than themselves, while trying with almost as much ardour to avoid those less powerful or wealthy from doing the same thing to them. This inverted parody of Dante's Inferno at the top of the alps would make any normal person nauseous to watch. The global elite have managed to recreate, for their own torment, the exact same stratification for which they are responsible at mass scale in the rest of the world, played out over cocktails at 1560 metres with acute precision and endless supressed or disguised humiliation. They regard other people as *means* and are richly rewarded for it.

We celebrate and promote leaders who can build a strong culture. I have touched repeatedly on the centrality of diversity to innovation. My experience and all the research I have looked at supports the relatively obvious idea that a diverse group will be both more creative and more attuned to diverse customer and citizen needs than a homogenous group-thinking executive team.[17] But many of our leaders have learned only that this is something that they ought to do for some kind of hazy reasons of fairness and social justice. There is a powerful fairness argument to be made that it is true but it's not relevant here, where we are focussed on effective strategy patterns. What we actually need is a diversity of thinking, which is a product of a diversity of culture, education, outlook and experience.

It will be apparent to the careful reader that many of the characteristics I have already listed above are partly instantiations of dominant groups and their cultures and it's probably as well to take this into account when judging your capacity to challenge them and the existential woe that you may be engendering in your leaders. The ways in which this plays out varies from country to country and sector to sector. But to illustrate a point that could equally be made about race or disability or any one of a number of intersecting vectors, let's dwell for a moment on gender and misogyny. Many may find it odd to see the subject of feminism and misogyny in the context of a book on innovation, but bear with me a minute because I believe it highlights something fundamental.

I have worked for several organisations that prided themselves on their understanding and rejection of sexism in all its forms. At one of them I had a very revealing experience. Several senior managers approached the Director of People asking for a gender breakdown of pay with variables for place, grade, longevity, etc. He expressed great shock at the request and assured us that this was the last organisation on earth that might have a gendered pay disparity issue, that they were devoted both as individuals and a management team to every kind of equality and particularly to feminism. We insisted that it might be useful and to his credit he carried out a very detailed analysis. Controlling for all the variables the difference was around 18 per cent (a little above the OECD average.) He was as shocked as we were and helped us find the money to fix the problem within 18 months: no mean feat for a resource-constrained organisation.

We learned several things from this experience. The framework I would place them in, I take from the work of brilliant fellow Australian, Kate Manne, currently professor of Philosophy at Cornell. Professor Manne argues that misogyny is not as many naturally assume a character defect but is, and always has been, about supporting and policing a system of control through rewards and punishments, and that looking for individual traits like 'hatred of women' while applicable in some isolated cases, generally misses most of what is going on. And as that other great Australian philosopher, Hannah Gadsby, has pointed out, allowing any powerful group to define their goodness against the badness of the rotten apples who 'crossed the line' leaves the power for drawing that line in exactly the wrong hands.

Like any self-sustaining system protecting the power of a particular group, it regenerates itself through a thousand subtle cues and expectations, myths and limitations, unwritten rules and learned behaviours. It is the system that when large groups of corporate employees are given identical CVs of a man and a woman, 86 per cent judge the man to be more 'competent' but both equally likeable. When competence is held equal by being told that both have been given the top performance ranking, 83 per cent then judge the man to be more 'likeable' (*Down Girl*, pp. 252–253; quoting research by Madeleine Heilman and others).

It is clear that many of the traits I've written about above are, among other things, evidence of exactly this kind of system at work. It is not enough to be 'in favour of fairness' or to 'love and respect women' or even to be 'a committed feminist' as several of my co-directors undoubtedly were. Like everything else I've written about here, you have to figure out how to actively and passionately pursue your objective.

The continuing act of innovation requires a love of the free choice, not only of those you aspire to innovate for but, of necessity, those who will build and lead your innovation team in pursuit of human flourishing. A sexist system policed by misogynistic cultural enforcement is a deterministic system (most although not all deterministic systems are misogynistic). Like the discredited deterministic justifications of racial correlations with IQ, or the spurious inevitability of algorithms in search and social networking, these power systems are nearly always the accreted architecture of constraint on the freedoms of one group for the obscured benefit of another. These dead and deadening systems of leadership we have too readily accepted also need to change. We have to innovate to innovate.

What then does great innovation leadership look like?

If we allow that free will is distinctively human and respect for it the root of human flourishing, we will commit firstly to not blocking people's exercise of it to become more fully human and secondly to actively encourage self-actualisation. This for me is the essential politics of innovation; it commits to both defending and enhancing autonomy. Taking this not only as the nature of purpose, but the actual purpose we will attempt to achieve, and turning away from the limiting approaches to leadership explored above, we arrive at some good, simple, workable principles to use in the conduct of our work and our leadership. Leadership is now understood to be the selecting, nurturing and empowerment of a group of people to become transformationally great through unlocking and beginning to explore and realise their extraordinary full potential. Not accidentally, these are the converse of the leadership selection criteria criticised above.

The great leader is therefore *open*. Open to the very different strengths of the very different people they recruit. Open to new possibilities and potentials, new combinations and new insights. Open to the lives and the needs and wants of their potential customers and citizens, open to the true ways and side ways of the world. Open to the possibility of better and more beautiful or sustaining futures.

Open to change their mind, open to learn, open to admit failure with grace. Open to real feedback. Genuinely open to examining their own, their team's and their organisation's failures. This is so hard to do and takes such grace and confidence. Most successful leaders are very good at examining other people's failures in the sense of scoring points by shedding some light on somebody else's fuckup. This is not what we mean by learning from failure. We mean giving our colleagues sufficient safety and incentive to be open about the ways in which we went wrong.

The great innovation leader ensures that their colleagues are empowered and encouraged to live balanced lives, to be good members of their families and communities and to enrich themselves intellectually, socially and culturally both in work and beyond. The open leader creates an environment in which their colleagues are permitted and encouraged to be open themselves.

In both the Nicomachean Ethics and in the earlier Eudemian Ethics, Aristotle gave a full, compelling account of how we could achieve the highest thing, a life lived well. Rejecting Plato's idea that virtues were qualities we could learn or directives we could discover, he pursued instead an idea that what we can learn is an approach and a disposition towards balance (the avoidance of excess or absence in a pleasure or activity) and the love of *kalon*, beauty and nobility as a purpose and the rejection of *aischron*, the ugly and shameful. I had an extraordinary philosophy teacher called Peter Herbst at the Australian National University who summed up this approach very simply as 'living a full, rich life involves both work and love, pleasures and struggles, learning and playing, drinking Mr Henschke's good wine, spending time with friends in good conversation and contributing to your community as an active citizen through politics or in some other way'.

A great innovation leader will create a culture of constant imminent celebration. Her respect for and celebration of each member of her team's contributions are natural and pervasive. Diversity and a shared sense of purpose create the conditions for celebration, and the leader ensures that there are pauses to stop and savour the achievements of both the individuals and the group. The rituals of celebration are a fundamentally human activity and always have been. Thus, work becomes fully a part of life and celebration of work becomes celebration of life. We stop destroying our free time by being always available and always to some degree at work and instead start enriching our work life with real life. The forms celebration rituals will take will vary from place to place and culture to culture. Californians tend to be always giving prizes, whereas the English are more likely to slope off to the pub. Great teams are *always* celebrating something.

But great leaders also set and maintain high standards. They tend to create a culture where people insist on and are obliged to take responsibility for their own shortcomings and failures, not just because it is safe to do so but because they know they will receive constructive support in dealing with them. Part of the problem here is that there are very many different kinds of failure, and failures have different meanings at different times and in different organisations or parts of the same organisation. Highly fault-intolerant processes are essential to many operations. But managers need to be able to create innovation spaces where failure is not just tolerated but understood to be essential to iterative experimentation and learning. And be able to distinguish between the failures that are deliberate and generative from those that are understandable because of complexity and both of those from failures that derive from ignorance of or deviance from critical accepted group norms. The group's esprit de corps relies on the leader to celebrate the former, tolerate the understandable and reject or sanction the latter.

This tripartite distinction is complex but important so an example may help to illustrate it. Imagine your innovation group was working to make cross-border trade more frictionless. A generative failure might involve bringing a new technology like radio frequency identification (RFID) to bear or perhaps redefining the problem by moving the border. A complexity failure may occur in attempts to automate or integrate the 30 parties, 40 documents and 200 data elements involved in a single average cross-border trade.[18] An ignorance or normatively deviant failure might involve suggesting that a hard border crossing is no more complex than, for example, moving between two parts of London on either side of the congestion charging line or, for that matter, claiming to have a new solution but keeping it secret from the other members of the team.

Edward Tufte has made great points about poor data visualisation opening organisations to risk but when he blames PowerPoint for the Columbia shuttle tragedy, I think he misses some critical points about the culture in NASA at that time. Research suggests that the threat NASA faced from the known foam strike on the launch of Columbia was ambiguous, which opened the way for natural tendency to hope for the best, combined with fear of reporting errors, compounded with groupthink to lead senior managers to repeatedly ignore requests from engineers for more information, which could have led to prevention of the tragedy.[19]

Innovation leaders create a shared understanding of and belief in the mission of the group, which means that the final outcome is always desired, and setbacks are identified and prevented. Innovation means walking into the unknown. This can feel like walking in the starless dark or walking off a cliff. Which is why we constantly turn to the reassurance of process, the comfort of repetition or the handholding of reassuringly overpriced consultants. But the right people with the right skills and the right shared purpose will know, if they rely on each other's collective wisdom, how to navigate the unknown.

One of the simplest ways to distinguish between a true leader and the rest is to ask yourself this simple question. Do they tend to take responsibility for their team's failures and give credit away for their successes or the opposite? I had an SVP at Cisco, Gary Bridge, who had distinctively perfected the art of being endlessly tolerant of well-motivated generative failures, which he protected you for making and carried the responsibility for in a highly fault-intolerant wider culture. Our success rate as an innovation group was somewhere in the vicinity of one on seven, which is reasonably typical as far as I can tell. When we did have a success he quickly stood back and said, 'it was them'. This of course depended entirely on his own sense of security and self-worth and the executive sponsorship he represented and maintained. The great innovation leader always tends towards taking responsibility for things that go wrong and giving all the credit to others for things that go right.

There is considerable research to show that most of us tend to have a self-serving attributional bias, blaming failure on uncontrollable external factors and success on personal hard work and brilliance. Some research suggests that this is particularly marked among men, a learned behaviour less apparent with children. This varies by culture and age. The careful, seasoned leader understands this and understands that self-confidence and self-belief are critical to peak performance. Navigating between inspiration and fairness, pragmatism and dreams, they provide a safe environment where difficult truths can be shared, and self-serving behaviours give way to those that are purpose serving.

It is worth noting that a group or individual that repeatedly fails or fails for the wrong reasons should be fired. Laziness, dishonesty, selfishness, aggression and deliberately creating negative group dynamics are all sackable offences in any well-managed group. It's perfectly clear that people tend to behave better the more they are trusted, but trust cannot be blind. The manager who turns away in fear from addressing the team member who does not carry their weight or undermines others is headed for trouble. The overall ROI on an innovation programme should be very high over the mid to long term. It's just that it's managed in a way to allow intensive experimentation, which looked at close up mostly looks like repeated failure. In the public sector, where you can't fire people and you can't be seen to fail, internal solutions, strongly managed, need to be found.

The innovation leader finds ways to persuade people that if we all knew how much we all know, we would be amazing. The outperforming group values deeply the skills and insights of every member of the group and overcomes the barriers created by the different languages and metrics that flow from their necessary diversity. As John Kao has highlighted, that is why they can perform with the discipline, mutual respect and freedom characteristic of a great jazz ensemble. There is a shared vocabulary and a shared understanding and a shared objective but each of the skills and histories is different, driven by the different disciplines each instrument demands and the different personal experiences and struggles of the individuals involved, not to mention the different but overlapping parts of the canon they have been most influenced by and most freely reference (plagiarise.)

There is a great scene in *West Wing* (Season 4, Episode 15), where President Bartlet tests his staff with the first half of a well-known quote from American cultural anthropologist, Margaret Mead: 'Bartlet: Never doubt that a small group of thoughtful and committed people can change the world. Do you know why? Will: Because it's the only thing that ever has.'

A great leader and her great team never try to solve a problem requiring good judgement or leaderly decisiveness or group creativity *with a process*. Processes are fundamentally important in the delivery of complex work, but they are tools that come after human judgement and give effect to it. The good leader understands the difference between the power of using processes to support good decision making and the more or less complete abrogation of responsibility that comes with relying on processes to justify decisions they are afraid to own or create, decisions they are afraid to make. This relates closely to the points made above about data. The intrusion of consultants equipped with MBAs into the modern organisation has been almost completely baleful in its effects for this reason. How many times have I seen an Executive Vice President, way out of his depth, knowing he needs to innovate and no idea where to start, turn to McKinsey or Bain or the like with a wheelbarrow full of cash? Asking a strategy consultant to help you innovate is like asking a fish to help you fly.

The responsibility to orchestrate collaborative, open and ultimately decisive decision making is central to the role of leadership, and the leader who turns away from it is no longer a true leader. Many leaders make the mistake of thinking that decisiveness on the one hand and adaptiveness, openness and consultation on the other are mutually exclusive leadership styles. Great leaders are very open, even when they are very driven. They change their minds. And, when the time is right, they are very decisive. Great leaders decide slowly and implement fast. Many organisations decide quickly and implement slowly. Or decide nervously and leave the decision open to repeated questioning, second guessing and undermining. This is not just corrosive to the leader's authority, but deeply undermines the team's commitment and productivity as they are acutely aware that the wind might change direction.

True leaders treat all people with respect and understand that great innovations are rooted in true human relationships and that all real relationships are non-transactional relationships.

Most organisations' strategies are based on a deep fear – the fear that other people know how to do this properly. There is a pyramid of fear. Roughly speaking, charities and other organisations in receipt of public money are forced to be so risk averse that they end up copying what their government sponsors were doing 10 years ago. For various political reasons, ministers have been convinced, explicitly or implicitly, that public sector organisations are much less efficient and innovative than private sector organisations – so they end up copying what companies were doing 10 years ago. Most companies are also terrified and the bulk of them end up copying what the most innovative and successful companies were doing 10 years ago (if they can't buy them). This means that the most critical organisations working right at the front line with communities are running about 40 years behind what the most innovative organisations are doing. (There are some great but rare exceptions to this.)

The most interesting and innovative organisations around at the moment, regardless of sector, have tended to turn this pyramid of fear on its head. They are learning how community-rooted, values-based, movement-like organisations and networks can be the basis for powerful innovation and change. This approach predates social networking and pervasive digital connectivity but has now in many cases brought these tools to bear in its purpose-driven, movement-making, inclusive, co-productive approach. I gave examples above of these two approaches, pre and post internet, in Basque and in Medellin. For a deep dive into some emerging examples of the latter type it's well worth a look at *New Power* by my brilliant former colleagues, Jeremy Heimans and Henry Timms. They explore the power of emerging (digital) movement trends. Increasingly decentralised, transparent, non-hierarchical and, critically, participative. Thus unlocking the passion that comes from helping to build something you care about, rather than just joining or getting employment at somebody else's approximation.[20]

But we have to slowly change a number of deeply rooted assumptions to harvest these insights with confidence.

Firstly, we need to free ourselves from the mechanistic, simplistic, damaging habit of imposing project management 'disciplines' and systems on things that are not projects. It's very hard to do this, to escape 'project thinking', especially in government, but it is surely vital. Project management is by its nature a hierarchical control mechanism perfect for predetermined, fault-intolerant implementation management. In environments like government and the third sector where pre-accountability for budget allocation is enforced, pretending to use project management is vital to securing funds. And yet it is particularly and increasingly inappropriate in the distributed environments spawned by the internet.

Interestingly, unnoticed by many working on the public and social side of the house until relatively recently, the software development world, which many think of as an archetype of project management thinking, has moved on from it to something much more like the approach described above. It is interesting and somewhat mournful that just as government discovers them, the various disciplines around agile and scrum-based programming have already started to ossify into the process-based arcana required by high-charging consultancies. You can pay a lot now to get agile methodology, yet much of how it is marketed as project management process runs counter to the brilliant original manifesto from the group that met in the Wasatch mountains of Utah in 2001.[21]

> **Individuals and interactions** over processes and tools
>
> **Working software** over comprehensive documentation
>
> **Customer collaboration** over contract negotiation
>
> **Responding to change** over following a plan

Secondly, we need to realise that the organisation is itself a network and work out the strengths and weaknesses of networks. The strength of a network is beautifully encapsulated in the original drawing on page one of the 1964 eleven volume report, 'On Distributed Communications', one of the foundation documents of the internet. Polish American engineer, Paul Baran, and RAND had been commissioned by the Department of Defence to think through from first principles how to create more resilient communications infrastructures.

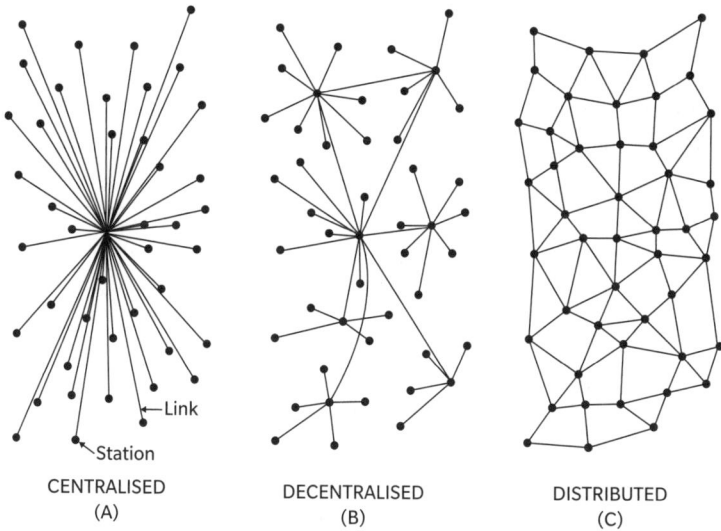

| CENTRALISED | DECENTRALISED | DISTRIBUTED |
| (A) | (B) | (C) |

One of the many ways to look at and understand the significance of Baran's drawings is to imagine them as organisations viewed from above. The first is a pure autocracy, the second a hierarchy, a set of government departments or company divisions perhaps and the third is a 'connected commons'. In the context of the recent slide of the US into kleptocratic autocracy it is worth observing the similarity between (A) above and Kurt Vonnegut's drawing of an arsehole in *Breakfast of Champions* (1973).

In its ideal form, a connected commons is resilient, distributed, equalitarian and collaborative by design. We can see modern instantiations of the idea in everything from Wikipedia to the 'Black Lives Matter' movement, the various sustainable cities networks and 'Me Too'. But these are Platonic forms and back on planet earth politics, the collective expression of our belief in free will intervenes.

The early hopes of the techno-utopians, myself among them, was that the introduction of the internet would open up the possibility of more inclusive, democratised organisations and institutions that empowered the edge and brought the centre under control or dissolved it altogether. But networks have many characteristics, and one is that 'rich nodes get richer'. Consider Twitter/X, Facebook or Amazon for three very different examples of the effect. The more people follow you on Twitter/X, the more people follow you on Twitter/X. The more your friends use Facebook, the less point there is using any platform that is not Facebook. And the more people shop from Amazon, the lower its per unit warehousing and logistics costs are than any possible competitor, an advantage it brilliantly transferred from stuff into the unexpected (probably even by them) adjacency of cloud storage space where the effects are even more marked. Add the huge time lag in taxation and privacy regulation as bordered governments struggle to keep up with the borderless new reality and we have a new set of political challenges as complex as any we have faced. Any serious innovation group or network needs to understand these new realities if they are to navigate implementations of the future.

On a side note, the extraordinary rise in Digital Public Infrastructures, driven by understandable sovereign fears of being unable to defend or preserve critical national economic infrastructure from various threats, has increasingly led to a different and, as yet, little understood threat from replacing very resilient distributed payments and data networks with very vulnerable and poorly governed centralised ones that are also anathema to innovation. It will be interesting to see which state succumbs first to narco-capture or some other form of kleptocracy due to not understanding the huge security and innovation rewards that have come from distributed networks.

Thirdly, we need to grasp that one of the fundamental keys to an innovative culture (and therefore to mission critical problem solving) is diversity. Diverse teams consistently outperform mono-cultural teams just as scientists from diverse faculties outperform those from specialised units when measured in Nobel prizes, for example, even though, ironically, the Nobel prize itself has a diversity problem (see this *HBR* article by Hewlett, Marshall & Sherbin).[22] This doesn't mean that you should go through some kind of pointless box-ticking exercise. It entails starting from a completely different outlook that comprehends that you will fail if your innovation group is homogenous. And it goes way beyond the normal categories of 'diversity'.

In fact, diversity is so central to this subject that it's worth taking a short detour to understand where we are at and where we are going wrong. The word itself has become problematic. Diversity for its own sake is proving increasingly counterproductive, even when measured by the lukewarm standards of some of those that advocate it. It even risks, as Angela Davis has argued, colonising and weakening the various struggles for justice that it purports to advance and becoming in the process capacious enough to become meaningless, while providing handy target practice for the increasingly emboldened bigots that are threatened by it. Worse still it can silently smuggle in an assumption of what is normal. We need an approach to building teams in which every member contributes to the diversity of that team, not because of how they look or pray or eat but more because of how they think. Diversity must itself have a purpose and a clearly defined one for the context in which you are seeking to innovate. It needs to take head on, break up and rebuild the very exclusions that are making us stupid. Nowhere is this more true than when we are innovating products, services or policies that serve wide, non-specialist populations; there are rich histories to be told of the endless errors made and commercial and political opportunities lost in serving forgotten segments of the population because they weren't represented at the various key stages of innovation. I remember arguing with a disability rights activist when I was running Motability that it was disingenuous to think we might redesign public infrastructure around the needs of the roughly 1 per cent of the population who use wheelchairs and she said, 'what about the roughly 60 per cent of the population who now or recently needed to push a baby in a buggy?' Neither group have traditionally been well represented and it sure as hell shows.

When working at start-ups I always had fun asking the diversity working group what their position on age was. I know you think I have a particular interest because I'm old, but actually I spent several decades of my career gaining unfair advantage from employing very, very experienced (old) folk. People at or near the end of their career have a huge number of things to offer the ambitious innovation-curious leader. Above all other things, they know a lot, not just about customers, citizens, etc., but also about what worked and failed, what failed for the wrong reasons, what never got tried for the wrong reasons, what traps lie ahead for the unwary, when colleagues need support or care but can't articulate it and so on. But that's not all! Old folk are generally dependable, don't need to be paid extraordinary amounts and, in an unexpectedly liberating swerve, aren't any longer seeking promotion and boundless appreciation and are thus liberated to collaborate, mentor, think long term (and strategise) in ways that are endlessly generous and generative. At one of the Silicon Valley start-ups I worked at where the average age was 26, the CEO called me up one day and asked 'Have you ever fired somebody?' Yes. Why? I replied. There was a long pause. 'How do you do that?'

Next, for models of transformational groups that have impact far beyond their size and that perform many times better than the norm, we need to think well beyond the conventions of corporatised 'high-performance team' management, which is hierarchical, process-based, pervasively normed and naturally Gaussian with statically defined roles; managed on the profound and damaging misconception that groups of people conform to averages with standard deviations rather than power law distributions with dramatic and disruptive outliers. Think for example of families, extraordinary musical ensembles, disruptive movements and tech start-ups. Each of these models can have disproportionate and transformational impact on individuals, communities and the world, but here are some of the things you will almost never find in them:

a. Regular, systematic performance appraisals.

b. Anything like a performance appraisal system that tells some large proportion of the group that they have under-performed the best.

c. Rigid and slowly changing hierarchies.

d. Job descriptions.

e. Weekly team meetings.

f. Performance-related pay and bonuses. (particularly ones that reinforce the message at (b) above that most of the team are under-performing.

g. Pay based on how many people you manage.

(See for example, 'Giving everyone an A' by the fabulous Benjamin Zander[23]).

In summary, it's worth dwelling on this profound point, that most outperforming small groups are distinguished by the fact that they treat their members as human beings, not resources. They treat each other as fundamentally equal, while diversely skilled and experienced. True equality never means similarity. What underpins this approach, as with all moral systems, is a view of what it is to be human. As I have argued here, that is some degree of free will, the spark without which there are no values, no meaning and no speech. The purpose of all purposes, that we are blessed with the divine power and inescapable responsibility to make the world better, fairer, more enjoyable and more just than it is. To reject the taught inevitabilities and exercise our free will in the expansion of the freedoms of others. Because as humans we are innovators.

Notes

1   Candela, Jacobsen & Reeves, MMCE, 2020.

2   Levinson, TB, Princeton University Press, 2006.

3   Stewart-Weeks, , AWTY, 2019.

4   Lack of broad support kills Croydon Tech City (techbritannia. co.uk) Techbritannia, 16 March 2018.

5   The work will apparently be in large part based on his PhD; Espiau, NVNSIP , 2022.

6   TBC, 2012.

7   This joke was stolen from the excellently named Simon Sinek.

8   Gatti, Irazusta & Albeniz, BS, 2017.

9   19 January 1989, during Whitehouse ceremonies awarding the medal of freedom.

10 Towards a Basque State, Citizenship and culture, Ipar Hegoa Foundation/Basque Summer University, 2012.

11 For a great analysis take a read of Peeters, Marc & Schoteten, Roel, LFMCM, 2024.

12 After shocking you with the news that Deming said the opposite of 'If you can't measure it you can't manage it', it should come as no surprise to discover that Peter Drucker never said 'culture eats strategy for breakfast'. According to the Drucker Institute, the closest he got was 'culture – no matter how defined – is singularly persistent'. The fact that he never said the thing he is most famous for saying is, I suppose, strong evidence for the theory that culture eats strategy for breakfast.

13 I'm deeply indebted to the brilliant and deep analyses of these phenomena carried out by Itziar Moreno and Gorka Espiau at the Basque Innovation Centre and for their kindness and patience in explaining them to me.

14 Gehry, El Pais, 2017, https://aboutbasquecountry.eus/ en/2017/09/03/frank-gehry-the-basques-keep-their-word-like- ive-never-seen-before/

15 https://deming.org/myth-if-you-cant-measure-it-you-cant-manage-it/

16 This argument is made much more eloquently by Dave Ulrich in 'A new mandate for human resources', *HBR* Jan–Feb 1998.

17 There are countless studies, but one that summarises and references several dozen pieces of peer-reviewed empirical research with clarity is: 'Does a different view create something new? The effect of employee diversity on innovation.' Ostergaard, Timmermans, Kristinsson, 2011, Aalborg University.

    A more recent literature survey can be found at 'Diversity, Innovation and Entrepreneurship: where are we and where should we go in future studies?', Karlsson, Rickardsson, Wincent, *Small Business Economics*, Springer, 2021.

18 https://blogs.lse.ac.uk/brexit/2019/02/06/long-read-there-is-no-such-thing-as-completely-frictionless-trade-across-a-border/

19 Roberto, Bohmer & Edmondson, FAT, 2006.

20 Timms & Heimans, NP, 2018.

21 https://agilemanifesto.org

22 https://hbr.org/2013/12/how-diversity-can-drive-innovation%20http:/www.diversityinc.com/diversity-management/proof-that-diversity-drives-innovation/

23 https://www.youtube.com/watch?v=qTKEBygQic0

chapter 7

———

60 propositions – for those too lazy to read books

This list contains a bunch of absurdly pithy propositions that might serve as a summary for the impatient, a quick reference or even, in part or in whole, a manifesto for the passionate. In this chapter I have sought to distil the fundamental points made in the rest of the book in as brief and succinct a way as possible. My aim is that this short list of propositions could be used both as a reminder or a refresher but also as a possible cheat-sheet or wall poster for those organising workshops, ideations sessions, working groups, task forces, etc.

1 Innovation is the sustainable, purpose-driven answer to a previously unsolved problem in the world.

2 There is no aspect of an organisation's business, operations, financing, approach to customers and citizens, communications or relationship to suppliers and partners that cannot valuably be the subject of innovation.

3 A successful innovation nearly always identifies a frustrated choice, perhaps one that is not yet even known, a frustrated opportunity to be more human.

4 Adding a shared purpose rooted in hard-won customer understanding to a diverse group of deeply skilled people is like throwing petrol on fire.

5 If you can't measure it, you may just be able to lead it.

6 Real leaders tend towards taking responsibility for things that go wrong and giving all the credit to others for things that go right.

7 The open leader creates an environment in which their colleagues know that they are safe to be open themselves.

8 The innovation leader finds ways to persuade people that if we all knew how much we all know, we would be amazing.

9 The outperforming group values deeply the skills and insights of every member of the group.

10 The leader's main job is to overcome the barriers created by the different languages and metrics that flow from their team's necessary diversity.

11 Welcome the chaos, embrace complexity, keep moving.

12 Question process.

13 Be deeply suspicious of implicit inevitability.

14 Proximity fosters serendipity.

15 Simplified lists like this don't do justice to the depth of innovation.

16 Stop thinking of innovation as a product or service; think of everything that surrounds the created product or service.

17 True innovation ultimately disrupts the norms of organisations.

18 Leaders could try a little harder to understand the resistance innovators face.

19 Frustrations are gold.

20 Innovation often means navigating constraints, not eliminating them.

21 Most innovations come from a series of small changes, not big leaps.

22 Copy ruthlessly and adapt carefully.

23 Innovation demands persistent execution.

24 Implementation is always the hardest part of innovation.

25 Without organisational adoption, an idea is just a dream.

26 Giving unearned credit to others is the innovator's secret currency.

27 Innovation doesn't have to be glamorous or pretty; it just has to work.

28 A one in seven success rate is a good rule of thumb for an innovation-focussed team. Failure is the fuel of future success.

29 Innovation isn't always about invention – it's often about recombination.

30 Look harder for unmet needs.

31 Great innovation teams are built, not born.

32 Innovation without purpose is just tinkering.

33 Purpose-driven innovation creates lasting change.

34 Understanding good design is essential to great innovation.

35 Innovation, like design, is the art of the endless trade-off.

36 Resist the urge to over-plan.

37 Great companies innovate to delight, not just to survive.

38 If your only goal is profit, you will fail to profit.

39 Disruption often begins with a simple solution to an overlooked problem.

40 Strategy serves purpose, not the other way around.

41 True innovation is about human flourishing.

42 Build an ecosystem of innovation, not just a team.

43 Cross-disciplinary teams generate the most creative ideas.

44 Don't get trapped by the binary of innovation vs. tradition.

45 Try breaking a simple habit. One at a time.

46 Innovators – rebels with a cause.

47 Corporate innovation isn't dead, it's just been locked in a cupboard somewhere.

48 Systems can support, but people innovate.

49 Lead with passion, not process.

50 Innovation should simplify, not complicate.

51 Most people overestimate the power of big ideas and underestimate the power of small ones.

52 Innovation is a series of calculated risks.

53 Great innovations often start with asking the right questions.

54 If it feels comfortable, you're not innovating enough.

55 The best innovations solve problems before they're obvious.

56 Epiphany + Perseverance = Poetry.

57 True innovators are always stupidly and annoyingly inquisitive.

58 Most outperforming small groups are distinguished by the fact that they treat their members as human beings, not resources. They treat each other as fundamentally equal, while diversely skilled and experienced. True equality never means similarity.

59 Anyone can innovate.

60 Breathe.

chapter 8

---

23 ½ practical workshop outlines

In this chapter I have created a set of practical workshop outlines that allow you to apply the patterns and insights of the previous chapters in a quick and practical way. The facilitator should have read the relevant chapters, but other participants need not – or may be directed to some pages in the preparatory reading created by the facilitator. In all cases you will need to be thoughtful about the representative nature of the participants. Are there underrepresented parts of the organisation present? How will you manage hierarchical, gendered or defensive behaviours? How will you ensure that the meek inherit the floor? None of these are set in stone and you should feel very free to play with timings, prompts, case studies, breaks and how to capture insights. In my own work I have ended up using elements of these around a structure for a several-days-long workshop that creates space for a carefully selected and very well-prepared group of people to walk through each of the stages I have described here so that they are able to ideate, heat map internal and external stakeholders, create the beginnings of a communication plan that should have elements of informing and persuading every month for the next two to three years and a detailed implementation plan with expert working groups properly resourced and staffed. And finally, and critically, a governance structure that ideally involves the CEO or at the very least those that report directly to them.

1 No product brainstorming bonanza (4 hours)

- Outcome: Actionable, non-product-based ideas for organisational improvement

- Overview: Participants brainstorm innovations that are not product based, but rather focussed on processes, organisational structures, management techniques, or other operational areas. By shifting focus away from product-based innovation, teams can discover new pathways for organisational growth and operational efficiency.

- Agenda:

  1 Introduction (30 mins): Facilitator explains the value of non-product innovation, sharing examples from companies

that succeeded by innovating business models or internal processes. Invite and discuss non-local examples from the group.

2 Team formation (10 mins): Break participants into groups (ideally cross-functional) and explain the task of banning product-related ideas.

3 Brainstorm session (90 mins): Each team brainstorms ways to innovate within recruitment, supply chains, management systems, etc.

4 Break (10 mins).

5 Plagiarising ideas (40 mins): Teams steal an idea from another group and improve upon it.

6 Presentations (40 mins): Each group presents their top idea and how they evolved it.

7 Debrief (20 mins): Teams discuss the importance of non-product innovation and the practicality of implementing the ideas.

2 Myth-busting innovation (2 hours)

- Outcome: A transformed understanding of innovation, with empowering beliefs replacing restrictive myths.

- Overview: Teams will work together to analyse and debunk common innovation myths (e.g., 'innovation is only for experts' or 'you need big budgets to innovate'). This process will help participants see how these beliefs stifle creativity and how they can cultivate a more inclusive culture of innovation.

- Agenda:

  1 Introduction (20 mins): The facilitator introduces common myths surrounding innovation.

  2 Team challenge (30 mins): Each group is assigned a myth and challenged with creating a presentation that debunks it using examples and research.

  3 Creative visualisation (30 mins): Teams create a visual representation (e.g., posters, infographics) illustrating the myth and its replacement.

4 Gallery walk (20 mins): Teams present their visual representations, with the audience providing feedback.

5 Debrief (20 mins): Teams discuss how these myths have impacted their organisational behaviour and how changing mindsets can help foster innovation.

3 The hero's journey of innovation (3 hours)

- Objective: Map the innovation journey using Joseph Campbell's *The Hero's Journey* to understand the phases of struggle, breakthrough and success.

- Outcome: Participants gain insight into the stages of innovation and strategies for navigating challenges effectively.

- Overview: Participants are invited to use the hero's journey as a metaphor for innovation, recognising that innovation requires overcoming obstacles and gathering allies, much like the hero of a story. This will help participants understand that anticipating and working around challenges and building alliances are a natural part of innovation and prepare them for strategic planning.

- Agenda:

  1 Hero's Journey overview (15 mins): The facilitator explains the Hero's Journey framework and its connection to innovation. The easiest way to do this is to get the participants to name their favourite films and then unpack them together.

  2 Story mapping (45 mins): Teams select one of their own organisation's breakthrough innovations or a well-known innovation (e.g., iPhone or Uber) and map its development against the Hero's Journey.

  3 Relating to your project (60 mins): Each team maps their own current innovation projects onto the Hero's Journey framework, identifying allies, challenges and expected outcomes.

  4 Group discussion (45 mins): Teams share their findings and discuss strategies for overcoming the 'challenges' phase.

5 Debrief (15 mins): Discuss the importance of embracing challenges and strategic risk-taking in the work of innovation.

4 Ethnographies of frustration (2 hours + field work +3 hours)

- Objective: Apply ethnographic research techniques to uncover frustrations and unmet needs of customers, employees or stakeholders.

- Outcome: Deep empathy with target users and actionable solutions based on real-world pain points.

- Overview: Teams will conduct rapid ethnographic research, observing behaviours and identifying frustrations that can fuel innovation. By understanding customer pain points and behaviours in real contexts, participants will develop usable ideas that address these challenges.

- Agenda:

  1 Introduction to ethnography (60 mins): The facilitator explains the principles of ethnographic research and its application to innovation.

  2 Preparation (60 mins): Teams identify target groups (customers, employees or stakeholders) and define their research objectives.

  3 Fieldwork: Teams conduct fieldwork, observing behaviours and interactions, and documenting frustrations or unmet needs. This can be done with real customers or service users or suitable proxies such as help desk staff, complaints service, quality control staff, front line service delivery or retail staff. Alternatively turn this into a one-day workshop by arranging for proxies to be available for a few hours on the day.

  4 Synthesis (60 mins): Teams regroup to discuss findings and identify key frustrations or unmet needs.

  5 Brainstorm solutions (60 mins): Based on the identified frustrations, teams brainstorm innovative solutions that address these needs.

6 Presentation (60 mins): Each team presents their findings and proposed innovations.

5 Pattern hunting for innovation (4 hours)

- Objective: Identify recurring patterns of success in innovation and apply them to new challenges within the organisation.

- Outcome: A clearer understanding of the kinds of patterns that contribute to innovation success and actionable strategies for applying these patterns to new projects.

- Overview: Participants will review successful case studies to uncover patterns that can be applied to their own projects. This structured approach to pattern recognition helps create a toolkit for teams to replicate successful innovation strategies.

- Agenda:

  1 Pattern introduction (30 mins): The facilitator introduces the concept of patterns in innovation and the value of recognising these patterns.

  2 Case study review (60 mins): Teams analyse successful innovations (e.g., Amazon Prime, Tesla, Skype, Dyson Vacuum Cleaners) to identify key success patterns (e.g., rapid prototyping, customer feedback loops, cross pollination, etc.).

  3 Pattern mapping (60 mins): Teams create a visual map of the patterns observed and how they contributed to the success of the case study.

  4 Application to current projects (40 mins): Teams apply these patterns to their current innovation challenges, identifying strategies that could work in their context.

  5 Presentations (30 mins): Each group presents their pattern maps and how they plan to incorporate these patterns into their projects.

  6 Conclusion (25 mins): Facilitator summarises common patterns across teams and discusses how these can be used as a toolkit for future innovations.

6 No assumptions allowed (4 hours)

- Objective: Challenge and dismantle the hidden organisational assumptions that inhibit innovation.

- Outcome: A set of innovative strategies that challenge existing organisational assumptions and open new pathways for growth.

- Overview: Participants are tasked with identifying and challenging long-held assumptions within their organisation that may limit creativity. Through this exercise, teams will learn to think beyond traditional constraints and explore new possibilities.

- Agenda:

  1 Introduction to assumptions (30 mins): The facilitator explains how assumptions can act as barriers to innovation and provides examples of companies that overcame these barriers (e.g., Netflix disrupting the traditional rental model).

  2 Assumption discovery (45 mins): Teams identify three to five assumptions within their organisation or industry (e.g., 'Customers will only buy in-store' or 'People won't pay for content' or 'Print is dead').

  3 Challenge the assumptions (45 mins): Teams brainstorm how to overturn these assumptions by asking 'What if the opposite were true?' and generating alternatives.

  4 Develop new strategies (60 mins): Based on the new perspectives, teams generate innovative ideas or strategies that break away from traditional assumptions.

  5 Break (45 mins).

  6 Presentations (60 mins): Teams present their new ideas and how they challenge existing assumptions.

  7 Conclusion (15 mins): The facilitator summarises key takeaways, highlighting how challenging assumptions can unlock innovative potential.

7 Reverse engineering fantasy football (4 hours)

- Objective: Work backwards from a successful end state to identify the steps needed to achieve breakthrough innovations.

- Outcome: A set of innovative strategies that challenge existing organisational assumptions and open new pathways for growth and experimentation.

- Overview: Teams are challenged to describe a perfect outcome, whether that be winning an industry award or launching a groundbreaking product. By reverse engineering the steps that would lead to this outcome, participants develop a practical roadmap for achieving success.

- Agenda:

  1 Introduction to reverse engineering (30 mins): The facilitator explains the concept of reverse engineering in the context of innovation and provides a real-world example (e.g., how Netflix reverse engineered its content recommendation system).

  2 Visioning success (30 mins): Teams define a perfect outcome for their organisation or product, whether it's market leadership, customer satisfaction or a major innovation award.

  3 Mapping the journey (60 mins): Teams work backwards from this perfect outcome, identifying key milestones and strategies needed to achieve each stage.

  4 Break (30 min).

  5 Identifying barriers (30 mins): Teams discuss potential barriers to success at each stage and brainstorm how to overcome them.

  6 Presenting the roadmap (30 mins): Each team presents its roadmap for achieving the perfect outcome.

  7 Conclusion (30 mins): Facilitator summarises the key learnings and discusses how this approach can be applied to ongoing projects.

8 Failure as fuel (screw-up Friday)

- Objective: Transform past failures into valuable lessons that drive future innovations.

- Outcome: A framework for learning from failure and actionable strategies for turning past mistakes into future successes.

- Overview: Participants will reflect on their previous failures, either personally or organisationally, and identify the root causes and lessons that can be applied to future projects. By embracing failure as a learning tool, teams will build resilience and foster an attitude of fondness for failure as the fuel of future success.

- Agenda:

  1 Introduction to productive failure (15 mins): Facilitator discusses how failure can lead to future innovation, using examples of famous failures (e.g., Apple Newton, Ford Edsel) that eventually resulted in major successes.

  2 Failure sharing (60 mins): Teams share personal or organisational failure stories, focussing on what went wrong and why.

  3 Root cause analysis (30 mins): Teams perform a root cause analysis of the failures, identifying the core issues and missed opportunities.

  4 Break (15 mins).

  5 Failure reframing (60 mins): Teams brainstorm how they can turn their failures into opportunities, exploring how the lessons learned can inform current or future projects.

  6 Presentation (30 mins): Teams present their 'failure-to-innovation' stories and proposed new directions.

  7 Debrief (30 mins): Discuss the importance of fostering a failure-positive culture in an innovation-driven organisation.

9 Creating platforms for change (4 hours)

- Outcome: Platform models that facilitate ongoing innovation through external collaboration.

- Overview: Participants will design platform models that allow for external contributors (e.g., customers, partners) to innovate within a company's framework. This encourages open collaboration and collective problem-solving.

- Agenda:

  1 Introduction to platform thinking (30 mins): Facilitator introduces the concept of platforms, using examples such as the App Store, Airbnb and open-source software.

  2 Define your platform's purpose (30 mins): Teams decide what their platform will enable users to do (e.g., share ideas, create products, access services).

  3 Platform design (60 mins): Teams design a basic structure for their platform, including rules, user roles and potential incentives for participation.

  4 Break (45 mins).

  5 Feedback loop design (30 mins): Teams brainstorm how they will collect feedback from platform users to improve and evolve the platform over time.

  6 Presentation (30 mins): Teams present their platform concepts and gather feedback from peers.

  7 Debrief (15 mins): Facilitator discusses how platforms can scale and sustain innovation beyond the organisation's internal capabilities.

10 Leadership innovation lab (4.5 hours)

- Outcome: Leadership strategies and principles that support an innovative, risk-positive organisational culture.

- Overview: This workshop focusses on empowering leaders to cultivate an innovation-friendly environment. Participants will explore leadership styles that encourage experimentation, risk-taking and collaborative problem-solving.

- Agenda:

  1 Introduction to leadership for innovation (15 mins): Facilitator discusses how leadership can enable or stifle

innovation, using real-world examples of innovative leaders (e.g., Ursula Burns, Satya Nadella, Laura Alber).

2 Leadership role-play (45 mins): Teams role-play different leadership scenarios that either encourage or hinder innovation. Each group takes turns playing the leader and the team, simulating various outcomes.

3 Break (45 mins).

4 Leadership strategy development (60 mins): Based on the role-play, teams develop a set of leadership principles for promoting innovation within their organisation.

5 Building an innovation culture (60 mins): Teams discuss how to create a culture that encourages risk-taking and experimentation without fear of failure.

6 Presentation (30 mins): Each group presents their innovation leadership strategies.

7 Debrief (15 mins): Facilitator discusses how leadership styles impact organisational innovation and provides tips for building resilient, innovative teams.

11 Agile in a day (2.5 hours)

- Objective: Understand and apply the fundamentals of agile methodologies to accelerate innovation.

- Outcome: Hands-on experience with agile processes, providing participants with a practical understanding of how agility can accelerate innovation.

- Overview: In this immersive workshop, participants will learn the core principles of agile methodology and experience a hands-on simulation of an agile project lifecycle, allowing them to understand how agility fosters innovation through iterative cycles and constant feedback.

- Agenda:

  1 Agile introduction (30 mins): Facilitator introduces the core principles of agile (e.g., iteration, sprints, scrums) and how agility can play an essential role in accelerating innovation.

2 Agile simulation set-up (30 mins): Teams are assigned a simple innovation challenge, which they will tackle using agile methods (e.g., designing a new feature or service).

3 Sprint planning (30 mins): Teams break down the challenge into smaller tasks and assign roles, setting up their first sprint.

4 Sprint execution (30 mins): Teams complete their tasks within a defined time frame (sprint) and then reconvene to review and adjust based on feedback.

5 Iteration and adjustment (30 mins): Teams repeat the sprint process, refining their innovation based on new insights or challenges.

6 Presentation (40 mins): Teams present their final output and reflect on the agile process.

7 Debrief (20 mins): Facilitator discusses how agile methodologies can be applied to ongoing projects in the organisation.

12 Collaborative prototyping sprint (3 hours)

- Objective: Rapidly prototype innovative ideas through collaboration and quick iteration.

- Outcome: Tangible prototypes with multiple iterations and a clear understanding of the role of prototyping in innovation.

- Overview: Participants will engage in a fast-paced prototyping sprint, where they will create low-fidelity prototypes based on specific challenges. Through feedback loops and iterations, participants will refine their ideas in real time.

- Agenda:

    1 Prototyping overview (30 mins): Facilitator explains the importance of prototyping and iteration in the innovation process, showing examples of low-fidelity prototypes from successful startups.

    2 Challenge introduction (10 mins): Teams are assigned a challenge (e.g., creating a new customer service experience or designing a new product feature).

3 Initial prototype development (30 mins): Teams create quick paper or digital prototypes to address the challenge, keeping the design simple.

4 Feedback round 1 (15 mins): Teams present their prototypes to another group and receive feedback.

5 Iteration (30 mins): Based on the feedback, teams refine their prototypes and make adjustments.

6 Final presentation (60 mins): Each team presents their refined prototype to the larger group.

7 Debrief (15 mins): Facilitator discusses how rapid prototyping and feedback loops can accelerate innovation and ensure better user alignment.

13 Inclusive innovation hackathon (5 hours)

- Outcome: Inclusive, innovative solutions designed to address underrepresented needs, and strategies to integrate inclusivity into everyday operations.

- Overview: Participants will work in teams to identify gaps in inclusivity within their industry or organisation and create innovative solutions to address these needs. This hackathon-style workshop will push teams to think beyond traditional customer bases and consider diverse perspectives.

- Agenda:

1 Introduction to inclusive innovation (30 mins): Facilitator explains how inclusivity drives innovation, using examples of companies that successfully integrated diverse perspectives into their product development (e.g., Microsoft's adaptive controller).

2 Team challenge (30 mins): Teams are tasked with identifying an area within their company or industry where inclusivity is lacking.

3 Brainstorming and ideation (60 mins): Teams brainstorm innovative solutions to address inclusivity gaps, considering accessibility, underrepresented customer bases or employee diversity.

4 Break (55 mins).

5 Prototyping (60 mins): Teams build a prototype or outline for their inclusive innovation solution.

6 Presentation (30 mins): Teams present their innovations to the group, highlighting how their ideas promote inclusivity.

7 Judging and feedback (20 mins): A panel of peers or experts evaluates the ideas based on criteria such as impact, feasibility and inclusivity.

8 Debrief (15 mins): Facilitator discusses how inclusive innovation can become part of the company's broader strategy.

14 Internal innovation Olympics (4 hours)

- Objective: Stimulate friendly competition to generate creative solutions and foster innovation.

- Outcome: Implementable solutions generated through engaging, competitive exercises, and a heightened sense of creativity and collaboration within the team.

- Overview: Teams will compete in a series of innovation challenges, designed to test their creativity and problem-solving abilities. These challenges will mimic real-world situations and push teams to think outside the box while developing actionable solutions.

- Agenda:

1 Introduction to innovation Olympics (15 mins): The facilitator explains the format and objectives of the competition, highlighting how creativity and collaboration will be rewarded.

2 Challenge 1: Business model innovation (30 mins): Teams are tasked with rethinking an existing business model for a well-known product or service.

3 Challenge 2: Process optimization (30 mins): Teams must innovate a specific internal process (e.g., supply chain, recruitment or customer service) to improve efficiency.

4 Challenge 3: Wildcard (30 mins): A surprise challenge is introduced, pushing teams to quickly adapt to new constraints.

5 Break (20 mins).

6 Presentation and judging (45 mins): Teams present their solutions to a panel of judges, explaining their rationale and expected impact.

7 Awards and feedback (20 mins): Winners are awarded based on creativity, feasibility and potential impact, followed by a feedback session.

8 Debrief (20 mins): The facilitator discusses how friendly competition can drive innovation and foster a culture of experimentation.

15 Skunk Works simulation (4.5 hours)

- Objective: Explore the power of small, elite teams to drive high-impact innovation.

- Outcome: A clear understanding of how Skunk Works teams can drive innovation, with a practical experience of rapid prototyping and problem-solving under constraints.

- Overview: Participants will simulate the creation of a 'Skunk Works' team – a small, autonomous team focussed on rapid innovation in a constrained, high-pressure environment. The simulation will show how these specialised teams can achieve breakthroughs in a fraction of the time of more conventional corporate or departmental approaches.

- Agenda:

  1 Introduction to Skunk Works (30 mins): The facilitator explains the concept of Skunk Works teams, referencing famous examples (e.g., Lockheed Martin's Skunk Works, Google X, UK Government's GDS before evisceration, Danish Government's Mindlab, before evisceration) and their role in innovation.

  2 Challenge assignment (10 mins): Teams are given a high-stakes challenge, such as designing a radical new product or

solving a major company pain point under significant constraints (e.g., time, resources or budget).

3 Rapid ideation (30 mins): Teams brainstorm and develop solutions, leveraging their autonomy and freedom to take risks.

4 Prototype development (45 mins): Teams create a simple prototype or model of their solution, focussing on proof of concept rather than perfection.

5 Break (20 mins).

6 Presentation and critique (60 mins): Teams present their Skunk Works prototypes and receive feedback from their peers and facilitator.

7 Reflection (60 mins): Teams discuss the advantages and challenges of working in a Skunk Works model and how these can be applied to their organisation.

8 Debrief (15 mins): The facilitator discusses how to establish and manage Skunk Works teams for ongoing innovation within an organisation.

16 Open challenge (3.5 hours)

- Objective: Explore the role of open innovation in creating solutions across sectors.

- Outcome: Cross-sector collaboration strategies and innovative ideas that leverage the strengths of multiple industries.

- Overview: Participants will develop a collaborative innovation project that spans multiple sectors (private, public and nonprofit). The workshop emphasises how cross-sector partnerships can yield groundbreaking innovations that no single sector could achieve alone.

- Agenda:

  1 Introduction to open innovation (20 mins): Facilitator introduces the concept of open innovation, showing examples of successful cross-sector collaborations (e.g., public–private partnerships for urban innovation).

2 Team formation and challenge assignment (20 mins): Teams are tasked with addressing a challenge that requires input from multiple sectors, such as climate change or social inequality.

3 Brainstorming session (45 mins): Teams develop ideas for their cross-sector innovation, identifying how each sector (private, public nonprofit) can contribute to the solution.

4 Break (15 mins).

5 Partnership strategies (60 mins): Teams outline how they would form strategic partnerships to bring their idea to life, including key stakeholders and potential obstacles.

6 Presentation (30 mins): Teams present their cross-sector innovation ideas, with a focus on the collaborative aspects and potential for societal impact.

7 Debrief and feedback (30 mins): The facilitator and peers provide feedback on the feasibility and creativity of the proposed solutions.

17 Customer/Citizen empathy mapping (one day)

- Outcome: Customer-centred solutions that address real needs, supported by deep empathy with the end-users.

- Overview: Participants will create empathy maps to better understand the emotional, psychological and practical needs of their customers. This workshop will focus on customer-centric innovation and how understanding customer pain points leads to better solutions.

- Agenda:

  1 Introduction to empathy mapping (30 mins): Facilitator explains the concept of empathy mapping, showing how it can lead to customer-focussed innovation (e.g., IDEO's design thinking approach).

  2 Customer research (120 mins): Teams gather customer data (through interviews, surveys or user personas) and begin

populating their empathy maps, noting what customers see, hear, think, feel and do.

3 Pain point identification (60 mins): Teams identify key pain points based on their empathy maps, focussing on unmet needs or frustrations.

4 Break (45 mins).

5 Solution ideation (60 mins): Using the pain points as a guide, teams brainstorm innovative solutions to address customer frustrations.

6 Prototype development (60 mins): Teams develop a quick prototype or outline of their customer-centred innovation.

7 Presentation (60 mins): Teams present their empathy maps and proposed solutions, explaining how they address customer needs.

8 Debrief (15 mins): Facilitator discusses how empathy mapping can be integrated into ongoing product development and service design work.

18 Innovation blindfold (2 hours)

- Objective: Push participants to think creatively by removing their sense of sight, forcing them to rely on other senses for problem-solving.

- Outcome: Enhanced creative thinking, with participants gaining a greater appreciation for non-visual problem-solving techniques and collaborative skills.

- Overview: In this interactive workshop, participants will engage in blindfolded problem-solving challenges, helping them unlock new ways of thinking. This exercise is designed to break habitual thought patterns and push participants out of their comfort zones.

- Agenda:

1 Introduction to sensory innovation (15 mins): Facilitator explains how removing sensory input can spark creativity by forcing people to rely on less dominant senses.

2 Blindfolded team challenge 1 (30 mins): Teams are blind-folded and tasked with solving a simple, tactile problem (e.g., assembling a puzzle or building a structure).

3 Challenge debrief (15 mins): Teams reflect on how relying on non-visual senses helped or hindered their problem-solving abilities.

4 Blindfolded team challenge 2 (30 mins): Teams tackle a more complex problem blindfolded, such as collaboratively designing a new product concept using only verbal communication.

5 Challenge debrief (15 mins): Teams discuss how removing sight changed their usual approach to problem-solving and teamwork.

6 Final reflection (15 mins): Participants remove their blindfolds and reflect on how sensory deprivation forced them to think differently.

19 Mission impossible ideation (2.5 hours)

- Objective: Tackle seemingly impossible challenges to spark breakthrough innovations. This exercise is less trivial than it seems as a way of disrupting unexamined inevitabilities.

- Outcome: Bold, unconventional ideas that challenge participants to think big and push the boundaries of what's possible.

- Overview: Participants will be given a set of 'impossible' challenges (e.g., achieving net-zero waste in five years, eliminating global hunger, finding a credible leader for the Tory party) and will be tasked with coming up with bold, out-of-the-box solutions. The focus is on pushing boundaries and exploring unconventional approaches to problem-solving.

- Agenda:

  1 Introduction to radical ideation (15 mins): Facilitator explains the importance of thinking beyond conventional limits, sharing examples of companies that tackled 'impossible' challenges (e.g., Gates malaria elimination, SpaceX's reusable rockets).

2 Impossible challenge assignment (15 mins): Teams are given an 'impossible' challenge related to their industry or a global issue.

3 Wild ideation (45 mins): Teams brainstorm wild, audacious ideas without constraints, generating as many ideas as possible, regardless of feasibility.

4 Break (15 mins).

5 Idea refinement (30 mins): Teams select their top three ideas and refine them, considering how they could be made more feasible.

6 Presentation (30 mins): Teams present their bold ideas, focussing on what makes their approach unique and how it challenges conventional thinking.

7 Feedback and debrief (30 mins): Teams receive feedback on their ideas, with the facilitator discussing how radical ideation can lead to transformative innovations.

20 Storytelling for innovation (4.5 hours)

- Objective: Use storytelling techniques to communicate innovation ideas and engage stakeholders. This should ideally be paired with other ideation, alliance building and communications exercises as the last stage of planning. It is profoundly important to the success of the other strands and is, in my experience, often underestimated or ignored. A properly crafted narrative will often be the main difference between the success and failure of a good idea.

- Outcome: Clear, compelling narratives that make innovative ideas more engaging and accessible to stakeholders.

- Overview: Participants will learn the art of storytelling as a way to communicate complex innovation ideas in an engaging and memorable way. They will practise building narratives around their projects to win buy-in from stakeholders.

- Agenda:

1 Introduction to Storytelling for Innovation (60 mins): Facilitator explains the role of storytelling in innovation,

using examples from successful startups and companies that excel at telling their innovation stories (e.g., Lego, DeepMind) and/or shows video examples of world-class story tellers to the group.

2 Story development (60 mins): Teams develop a narrative around one of their current innovation projects, focussing on the journey of the idea from inception to its future impact.

3 Break (25 mins).

4 Story refinement (30 mins): Teams refine their stories, ensuring they are clear, compelling and memorable.

5 Presentation (30 mins): Teams share their stories with the group, receiving feedback on how engaging and effective the narrative is.

6 Feedback and iteration (30 mins): Teams iterate on their stories based on feedback, making adjustments to improve clarity and impact.

7 Final presentation (20 mins): Teams present their final narratives to the larger group, focussing on how the story enhances the innovation's appeal to stakeholders.

8 Debrief (15 mins): Facilitator discusses the importance of storytelling in securing buy-in for innovative ideas and how to integrate storytelling into everyday project development.

21 Innovation through constraints (2.5 hours)

- Objective: Foster creativity by working within strict constraints.

- Outcome: Creative, resource-efficient solutions developed within strict constraints, with teams learning to embrace limitations as a driver of innovation.

- Overview: This workshop demonstrates how innovation can thrive under constraints by challenging participants to create solutions with limited resources, time or tools. By embracing limitations, teams will learn to think creatively and efficiently.

- Agenda:

  1 Introduction to constraints and innovation (15 mins): Facilitator explains how constraints can drive innovation, using examples such as NASA's Apollo 13 mission or companies like Airbnb that innovated with limited resources. Look alternatively at governments, particularly local governments that have operated in very resource constrained environments to reach surprising innovations. Basque, Brazil and Liberia come immediately to mind but there are many others.

  2 Challenge assignment (15 mins): Teams are assigned a challenge (e.g., designing a low-cost product or creating a solution within a strict time limit) and provided with specific constraints (e.g., limited budget, materials or time).

  3 Brainstorming and ideation (30 mins): Teams brainstorm solutions within their given constraints, focussing on maximising creativity with minimal resources.

  4 Prototype development (45 mins): Teams develop a quick prototype or outline of their solution, adhering strictly to their constraints.

  5 Presentation and critique (30 mins): Teams present their solutions and receive feedback on how they leveraged constraints to innovate.

  6 Debrief (15 mins): Facilitator discusses the role of constraints in fostering innovation and how teams can continue to embrace limitations as opportunities for creative problem solving.

22 Rapid experimentation lab (3.5 hours)

- Outcome: Practical experience with rapid experimentation, helping teams quickly test and iterate on their innovation ideas.
- Overview: In this hands-on workshop, participants will design and run rapid, low-cost experiments to test their innovation ideas. This iterative approach will help teams learn quickly and refine their ideas based on real-world feedback.

- Agenda:

  1 Introduction to rapid experimentation (15 mins): Facilitator introduces the principles of rapid experimentation, with examples of companies that use this method (e.g., Dropbox's MVP, Google's A/B testing).

  2 Experiment design (45 mins): Teams select an innovation idea and design a rapid experiment to test its feasibility. They outline the hypothesis, key metrics and success criteria for the experiment.

  3 Experiment set-up (30 mins): Teams set up their experiments, ensuring they can gather data quickly and make adjustments as needed.

  4 Execution and data collection (45 mins): Teams run their experiments, collect data and make real-time adjustments based on feedback.

  5 Analysis and iteration (30 mins): Teams analyse the results of their experiments and brainstorm how to iterate on their ideas based on the data they collected.

  6 Presentation and reflection (30 mins): Teams present their experiment results and discuss how rapid experimentation helped them refine their ideas.

  7 Debrief (15 mins): Facilitator discusses how rapid experimentation can be integrated into the innovation journey for ongoing learning and refinement.

23 Innovation ecosystem mapping (3 hours)

- Objective: Visualise and build an innovation ecosystem that supports long-term growth and collaboration.

- Outcome: A set of practical adoption and implementation alliances. A clear, practical map of the organisation's innovation ecosystem, with strategies to strengthen partnerships and leverage external resources for long-term innovation success. This exercise, performed in one way or another, is critical to success.

- Overview: Participants will map out their organisation's innovation ecosystem, identifying key players, resources and connections that support innovation. This workshop helps teams understand how to leverage external networks, partnerships and internal resources to create a thriving innovation ecosystem. I would suggest two different versions of this critical exercise for internal and external systems although a mapping within and beyond the company or department could also be undertaken – perhaps with two stages and a little extra time.

- Agenda:

  1 Introduction to innovation ecosystems (15 mins): Facilitator explains the concept of innovation ecosystems, with examples from companies that built thriving ecosystems (e.g., Apple's developer ecosystem, Amazon's logistics network).

  2 Ecosystem mapping (45 mins): Teams map out their current innovation ecosystem, identifying key internal and external players (e.g., customers, suppliers, partners, investors) and how they interact.

  3 Gap analysis (30 mins): Teams identify gaps or weaknesses in their ecosystem, such as missing partnerships, underutilised resources or weak connections.

  4 Ecosystem strengthening (45 mins): Teams brainstorm how to strengthen their ecosystem by building new partnerships, optimising resources or creating stronger connections between different parts of the ecosystem.

  5 Presentation (30 mins): Teams present their ecosystem maps and strategies for strengthening their innovation networks.

  6 Debrief (15 mins): Facilitator discusses how a strong innovation ecosystem can support sustained growth and collaboration.

Annex A

A note on free will

'As human beings, our freedom lies in other kinds of rule- following, as well as revision, creation, breakage, and reformation.'

Kate Manne (DG, p. 30)

I have committed a number of philosophical sins in the creation of this essay. But several stand out. The first is to assert without proof that free will exists. The second, that it underpins the possibility of giving sense to language, meaning and value. The third that it is **a** or even **the** distinctively human characteristic, the attribute more than any other that makes us human. The fourth and possibly most egregious, that we could in some way derive values from facts, an 'ought' from an 'is' by implying that these facts, if that is what they are, can in some way build a foundation for giving moral value to the defence and encouragement of activities that respect and give amplitude to free will.

These are not unusual or even, God forbid, original philosophical sins. And I would have been comfortable committing them without defence if it were not for the recent popularity of some alternative views and the observable fact that several of my children seem to have fallen for the seductively readable intellectual marketing non-sense of Sam Harris and his ilk.[1] Most people will be comfortable with them, indeed most people clearly believe most of them if we take their behaviour as a guide. But for those who have a philosophical discomfort with this approach, I have added here not an argument, but a few comments. If you are like most people and perfectly comfortable with the idea that you can freely choose whether to have coffee or tea in the morning, then don't waste any more of your valuable time reading this annex.

You can try, if you want to be driven to despair, reading contemporary philosophers on this subject. The extent and complexity of their writing seem to be in inverse proportion to the boldness and creativity of their ambition. Mostly they are just like a European Institutional negotiation, impossible to follow and ultimately just kicking Lacan down the road, to steal a joke from my neighbour, Adrian.[2]

What would the alternative be and what are some things that would be true if the world had no free will in it? The main proposed alternatives are that everything is determined by chains of physical causality, that everything is random or, most popular, some mix of the two.

But surely science and the social sciences have made huge inroads into free will? We now know that our environment, our genes, our politics and a thousand other things actually determine much of what we think of as choices. Yes indeed. And there is nothing that a social scientist in search of tenure or a quick buck loves more than proving how stupid people are. Sadly, the onward march of the 'free' market into higher education and its lamentable effect on the value of cheap counterintuitives have done almost as much damage to thinking as organised religion did to metaphysics. But we don't need all actions to be freely willed or even most. We just need that last little sliver of autonomy to preserve human understanding.

We have to turn Kant upside down to get started. In other words, we must reject his idea that choices made from desire are not free, while those made by the application of reason are. We don't need to worry just now about the interesting reasons why he got these two back to front.

Every action is driven by a mixture of chance, desire, reason, history, biology, chemistry, society, genetics, etc. For our purposes we can divide these into three categories, the random (chance), the determined (history, biology, chemistry, society, genetics, etc.) and the rest. The question we are trying to answer is whether there is anything left after we have accounted for the determined and the random.

But it's a huge leap from saying that if there is nothing left to account for in explaining our actions after the random and the (physically and socially) determined have been given their full due, that we have excluded reason and thus the possibility of making true statements. And what if that were true anyway? What if we had excluded the possibility of making meaningful statements but that's just the way the world is and bad luck?

Well at that point we fall headlong into the infinitely meaningless void.

Every single act we take as individuals or families or workers or other communities or groups, to stop a wrong, from shooting an intruder or a dictator to petitioning or voting or marching on the legislature, is a single or collective expression of autonomy, the manifestation of our profoundly human rejection of inevitability. Every bloody step we take, if it's a free step, is an insult to inevitability. And every oppressor, from the husband who assaults his wife to the kleptocratically funded autocrat, attempts through lies, confusion, threats, coercion and violence to persuade us in some way or other that we have no choice. Because of historical determinism or the operation of the free market or national pride or manifest destiny or the dictates of nature or an inexplicable dislike of certain kinds of sex and not others.

All fundamental wrongs are rooted in limitations on our autonomy, and all fundamental rights are in some way an expression of opposition to that. It is in the nature of right and wrong behaviour that it has to express or limit autonomy. This is sometimes easy to work out and sometimes hard. And its hardest when one freedom conflicts with another. Like free speech and freedom from fear and persecution. So we have to accept some measure of free will exists or accept a howling and meaningless void of inevitability. It's a choice.

Notes

1 For a proper critique of Harris, one serious approach has been taken by Daniel Dennett. There are many others.

2 Sorry Ade. I couldn't help it.

Annex B

How to do start-ups

'I don't know about you people but I don't want to live in a world where someone else makes the world a better place, better than we do.'

(Silicon Valley, 2014)

Start-ups are one fundamental innovation vehicle that lie at the heart of the innovation ecosystem and thus our future well-being. Working in start-ups has been one of the highlights of my professional life: high energy, brilliant creative people, mission driven and all wrapped up in the excitement of knowing that you are inventing some slice of the future. It's not part of this essay's purpose to analyse start-ups and there are many fabulous books that do. But it's worth making a few comments in the light of the patterns we are looking at. I've worked at three start-ups and I have learned that you have to do some or all of the following things.

You must have a Foosball table. This one is actually compulsory, although there is no need for anyone to play on it. You should have some very strange chairs in retro colours, unlike all your other chairs as this fosters creativity. You should also have a vast array of free snacks curated on the assumption that your employees will either have the same tastes they had when they were 12 or that they are furry tree-dwelling mammals. You should have zones where people can meditate or play music or such like. Nobody will do these things, but it will make them more creative knowing they are there.

Your desks should be packed into a huge industrial open-plan space that looks like a factory and ideally actually was a factory that made real things in the past. This has the dual benefits of making people feel both cool and industrious while ensuring that they can't hear themselves think or have conversations about anything commercially sensitive, personnel related or, for that matter, personal. Don't dwell on the strange fact that your parents or grandparents devoted their lives to getting out of having to work in buildings like this – it's back to the factory floor for you student debt mules.

Some of your most senior people may find this working environment intolerable, and for them you should carve out little private offices in the corners of the industrial space. This has the added benefit that they will become inaccessible to their own staff and unaware of their emerging concerns and troubling dynamics flowing through the main working group. If you feel a little squeamish about the unequal treatment, it might be a good idea to call these offices 'meeting rooms' as in 'Ms CFO's meeting room' or 'Mr CEO's meeting room'. They can still be used like ordinary offices, but it looks less offensive to the staff.

You should base this space in the middle of the most expensive real estate cluster you can find like the SOMA district in San Francisco, the Flatiron quarter in Manhattan (Silicon Alley), Shoreditch in London (Silicon Roundabout), central Boston and the red line corridor or Silicon Allee and other parts of central Berlin. Of course, Berlin is cheaper, but you pay for that in lower clustering benefits.

This will allow you to maximise early investor cash burn both on accommodation costs and, even more, on engineer salaries where cost of living and competition with larger high-paying companies will ensure sky-high wage bills. It has the further benefit that your staff will never want for exciting things to do and coffee to drink should they get bored of playing Foosball and nibbling on cookie crisps as the afternoon drags on.

Make sure you hold a lot of meetings, not on the basis of who needs to be there to get to rapid and accurate decisions, but on who will be offended if they are not invited. Some senior engineers may baulk at this but most senior people won't, thus ensuring that your most seasoned and expensive staff are tied up in unproductive activity for long swathes of quality time.

If you have very talented members of staff who are good at creating visual analytics, get them to generate vast amounts of preparatory work for these meetings. This is a double win as it takes key junior resource away from making the business thrive as well as making the executive meetings much longer and more analytically exhausting and complex.

When mistakes are made, as they inevitably will be, instead of fearlessly working out why and who was responsible, allow executives the expedient of blaming the lack of some previously unthought-of visual analytics report. This slowly amplifies the effect of the previous point over time until you are likely to have to hire more analysts and the executive meetings go all day. It also ensures the same kinds of mistakes can be made repeatedly as they are almost never the fault of a lack of analytics report but something too hard to deal with, like a basic flaw in the business model or weak management.

While we are on the subject of substituting process for creativity and leadership, try to drive out or automate all creativity and design with as many A/B tests as you can physically do. Sure, it's true that no beautiful, startling or crazy new thing in the history of the world was arrived at through exhaustive A/B testing, but at least you can stop worrying about your lack of creativity and fall back on a rigorous numerically analysable process.

And on the sales side, make sure that everyone has to use Salesforce. Ideally over-specify unique requirements for your own company as this will be costly in itself both in retooling and retraining as well as absolutely maximising the time each rep has to spend wading through the mud of this already impossibly badly designed software uploading from his own personal spreadsheets in the post-hoc pretence that he has been using SFDC to track his sales activity through the absurd 12-stage process his head of sales imposed. This is a particularly valuable distraction for anyone involved in complex, high-value, long-cycle sales as they will have to continually over-write their previous absurd predictions and commits. Don't be deterred by the fact that you only have five products and 10 staff from letting the SFDC ops manager create literally thousands of stock-keeping units (SKUs) so that SFDC redundant re-inputting downtime can be maximised while harassed reps spend hours or even days trying to find the right product description.

Try to get people into management positions who are uniquely ill-qualified to manage human beings by virtue of extreme aggressiveness, unpleasant sexism or some other character flaw. Compensate for this by instituting a rolling programme of complex, compulsory, child-like team building activities like go-kart racing, beach volleyball, rock climbing, 80s-themed BBQs and the like. This has the dual benefits of consuming vast amounts of time and money and making sure that at least 35 per cent of your staff feel either frightened or humiliated by the atmosphere of aggressive competition masquerading as compulsory 'fun'. Make sure the aforementioned managers are visibly present, dressed in a fun age-inappropriate way and hugging people a lot to keep them totally on edge.

Try to keep fresh and disruptive thinking to an absolute minimum by ensuring that over 90 per cent of your staff are around about the same age and come from the same two or three academic backgrounds, wear the same clothes and have the same wacky taste in children's snacks, underwater polo and the like. Reassure yourself that you have employed both Asians and women and even some who are both. If this isn't enough to quell doubts about diversity, set up a staff working group on diversity. Don't include age as a parameter as it will make the staff jumpy. Execute via Slack.

Speaking of which, try to make sure that every member of staff is signed up to multiple work-related and non-work-related Slack channels. Talk a lot about how you don't even know how people did collaboration before Slack and laugh at Microsoft Groups. This has the benefit of virtualising collaboration and digitising human interactions, which in a small start-up sitting in one industrial room is, after all, very physically challenging. It has the added advantage that literally every member of the company will be interrupted by something unrelated to what they are working on every 90 seconds, thus ensuring that they never indulge in the dangerous habits of sustained thought, creativity or problem solving or challenged with the complex nuances of three-dimensional human conversation.

Try and ignore most of the useful detail in Lean Start-up methodology, which is complex and time-consuming to master, and focus instead on the two terms you can remember from the *HBR* or *Fast Company* article you read about it, The *Minimum Viable Product* and the *Pivot*. Don't waste a lot of time understanding your customers too deeply but get an MVP out into the marketplace quickly to ensure that your actual and potential competitors can learn cheaply from your early development work and replicate what works. That will ensure that you have to move very quickly to the Pivot as you have basically destroyed your appropriability and have to start again, thus hitting your two key targets in minimum viable time.

And remember, you won't need good design because your founder is way cool and has good taste by definition. And if he doesn't, it wouldn't be safe to tell him anyway because he most likely has a kind of driven, raging, supressed father-issues thing going on and is prone to act, even when implicitly criticised, like a cross between a minor medieval war-lord and a starving, passive-aggressive child.

Bibliography

Adrià, Ferran, *A Day at El Bulli*, Phaidon, 2008.

Adrià, Ferran, *Notes on Creativity*, published on 22 January 2014, The Drawing Center's Drawing Papers Volume 110 featuring a conversation between Brett Littman and Ferran Adrià and an essay by Richard Hamil.

Alexander, Christopher, Ishikawa, Sara & Silverstein, Murray, *A Pattern Language. Towns, Buildings, Construction.* Oxford University Press, 1977.

Alexander, Christopher, *The Timeless Way of Building*, Oxford University Press, 1979.

Baran, Paul, *On Distributed Communications*, Rand Corporation, California, 1964.

Bason, Christian, *Leading Public Sector Innovation*, 2nd edition, Policy Press, 2018.

Berlin, Isaiah, *Two Concepts of Liberty*, Oxford University Press, 1969.

Brand, Stewart, 1972-12-07 Rolling Stone (Excerpt) Spacewar Article 600DPI : Free Download, Borrow, and Streaming : Internet Archive.

Campbell, Joseph, *The Hero's Journey*, Harper Collins, 1991.

Candela, Rosalino A, Jacobsen, Peter J & Reeves, Kacey, 'Malcom McClean, containerization and entrepreneurship,' *The Review of Austrian Economics*, October 2020.

Cappelli, Peter & Tavis, Anna, 'The performance management revolution', *Harvard Business Review*, October 2016.

Chase, Robin, *Peers Inc: How People and Platforms Are Inventing the Collaborative Economy and Reinventing Capitalism*, Public Affairs, 2015.

Deschamps-Sonsino, Alexander, *Creating a Culture of Innovation*, Apress, 2020.

Drucker, Peter, *Innovation and Entrepreneurship*, Harper, 1985.

Espiau, Gorka, *Norms, Values and Narratives Social Innovation Processes. The Cultural Dimensions of the Socio-Economic Transformation of Basque Society* (1978–2022) EHU/UPV, Eusko Jaurlaritza, 2022.

Farage, Nigel, *The Guardian*, 3 July 2024.

Galbraith, John Kenneth, 'Let us begin', *Harper's Magazine*, March 1964.

Galloway, Scott, *The Four: The Hidden DNA of Amazon, Apple, Facebook and Google*, Bantam, 2017.

Gamma, Erich, Helm, Richard, Johnson, Ralph & Vlissides, John, *Design Patterns: Elements of Reusable Object-Oriented Software*, Addison-Wesley, Boston, 1994.

Gatti, Gabriel, Irazusta, Ignazio & Albeniz, Iñaki Martinez de, *Basque Society: Structures, Institutions, and Contemporary Life*, University of Nevada Press, 18 May 2017.

Gigerenzer, Gatti, 'The bias bias in behavioral economics', *Review of Behavioural Economics*, December 2018. https://www.nowpublishers.com/article/Details/RBE-0092

Goffman, Alice, *On the Run: Fugitive Life in an American City*, University of Chicago Press, 2014.

Heimans, Jeremy & Timms, Henry, *New Power: How Power Works in Our Hyperconnected World – and How to Make It Work for You*, Penguin, 2018.

Hiltzik, Michael A, *Dealers of Lightening. Xerox Parc and the Dawn of the Computer Age*, Harper Collins, 1999.

Ibarretxe Markuartu, Juan José, *The Basque Case: A Comprehensive Model for Sustainable Human Development*, Universidad del Pais Vasco, 2012.

Johar, Indy, *Compendium for the Civic Economy*, Valiz: Trancity, 2011.

Johnson, Steven, *Where Good Ideas Come From*, Riverhead, 2010.

Kahneman, Daniel, *Thinking Fast and Slow*, Farrer, Straus, Giroux, 2011.

Kao, John, *Innovation Nation*, Free Press, 2007.

Kelley, Tom, *The Ten Faces of Innovation*, Doubleday, 2005.

Klein, Ezra, *Sam Harris, Charles Murray, and the Allure of Race Science*, Vox, 27 March 2018.

Kocienda, Ken, *Inside Apple's Design Process During the Golden Age of Steve Jobs. Creative Selection*, St Martin's Press, 2018.

Koller, Tim, 'Are share buybacks jeopardising future growth'? McKinsey, October 2015.

Lazonick, William, 'Profits without prosperity', *Harvard Business Review*, September 2014.

Levinson, Marc, *The Box. How the Shipping Container Made the World Smaller and the World Economy Bigger*, Princeton University Press, 2006.

Lisa, McKenzie, *Getting By: Estates, Class and Culture in Austerity Britain*, Policy Press, 2015.

Machiavelli, Niccolo, *The Prince*, 1532.

Manne, Kate, *Down Girl: The Logic of Misogyny*, Penguin, 2017.

Markovits, D, *The Meritocracy Trap*, Penguin Ransom House, 2019.

Mazzucato, Mariana, *The Entrepreneurial State*, Anthem, 2013.

Mazzucato, Mariana, *The Value of Everything: Making and Taking in the Global Economy*, Allen Lane, 2018.

Mulgan, Geoff, *The Locust and the Bee*, Princeton University Press, 2013.

Nelson, Fraser, 'The return of eugenics', *The Spectator*, 2 April 2016.

Oliver, Scott, *The Fundamental Errors of Jordan Peterson*, Vice.com, 04 June 2018.

Peeters, Marc & Schoteten, Roel, *Lessons From the Mondragon Cooperative Movement*, Corporate-Rebels.com, 26 May 2024.

Perez, Carlota, *Technological Revolutions and Financial Capital*, Edward Elgar, 2002.

Rich, Ben & Janos, Leo, *Skunk Works*, Little Brown, 1994.

Rising, Linda & Manns, Mary Lynn, *Fearless Change: Patterns for Introducing New Ideas*. 2004.

Roberto, Michael, Bohmer, Richard M J & Edmondson, Amy C, *Facing Ambiguous Threats*, *Harvard Business Review*, November 2006.

Roston, Tom, ' *They Thought It Was Black Magic': An Oral History of TiVo – How the Original DVR Paved the Way for Netflix and the Cord-Cutter Movement*. OneZero, Medium, 2 Apr 2019.

Sanders, Michael, Stockdale, Emma, Hume, Susannah & John, Peter, 'Loss aversion fails to replicate in the coronavirus pandemic: evidence from an online experiment', *Economics Letters*, 199: 109433, 2021.

Sanders, Michael, Stockdale, Emma, Hume, Susannah & John, Peter, 'Nudge in the time of coronavirus: the compliance to behavioural messages during crisis', *Journal of Behavioural Public Administration*, 4(2), 2021.

Schumpeter, Joseph A, *Capitalism, Socialism and Democracy*, 2nd edition, Harper, 1947.

Sennett, Richard, *Together: The Rituals, Pleasures and Politics of Cooperation*, Allen Lane, 2012.

Sinek, Simon, How Great Leaders Inspire Action, *TedX Puget Sound*, 26 June 2013.

Snyder, Tim, *The Road to Unfreedom*, Tim Duggan Books, 2018.

Snyder, Tim, *On Freedom*, Penguin, 2024.

Sodha, Sonia, 'Nudge theory is a poor substitute for hard science in matters of life or death', *The Guardian*, 26 April 2020.

Stewart-Weeks, Martin, *'Are We There Yet? The Digital Transformation of Government and the Public Sector in Australia'*, Longueville Media, 2019.

Techbritannia, Lack of broad support kills Croydon Tech City (techbritannia.co.uk) Techbritannia, 16 March 2018.

Theil, Peter, *Zero to One*, Crown Business, 2014.

Timms, Henry & Heimans, Jeremy, *New Power: How It's Changing the 21st Century – and Why You Need to Know*, Macmillan, 2018.

Wiener, Anna, *Uncanny Valley*, Fourth Estate, 2019.

Wilkinson, Will, *The Freedom Lover's Case for the Welfare State*, Vox.com, 1 September 2014.

Vonnegut, Kurt, *Breakfast of Champions*, Delacorte Press, 1973.

Wittgenstein, Ludwig, *Culture and Value*, Georg Henrik von Wright (Editor), Peter Winch (Translator), University of Chicago Press, 1984.

Young, Michael Dunlop, *The Rise of the Meritocracy*, Pelican, 1958.

Zečević, Matej, Willig, Moritz, Singh Dhami, Devendra & Kersting, Kristian, 'Causal parrots: large language models may talk causality but are not causal', *Transactions on Machine Learning Research*, 2023.

Index

___